Religions
of the World

Buddhism

Patricia D. Netzley

Lucent Books, Inc.
10911 Technology Place, San Diego, California, 92127

On Cover: Inle Lake, monks nursing cats.

Titles in the Religions of the World series include:

Buddhism

Confucianism

Hinduism

Islam

Shinto

Library of Congress Cataloging-in-Publication Data

Netzley, Patricia D.
    Buddhism / Patricia D. Netzley.
        p. cm. — (Religions of the world)
Includes bibliographical references and index.
    ISBN 1-56006-983-X
I. Title. II. Religions of the world (San Diego, Calif.)
BQ4032 .N47 2002
294.3—dc21

2001005250

Copyright 2002 by Lucent Books
10911 Technology Place, San Diego, California, 92127

Printed in the U.S.A.

Contents

Foreword

Religion has always been a central component of human culture, though its form and practice have changed through time. Ancient people lived in a world they could not explain or comprehend. Their world consisted of an environment controlled by vague and mysterious powers attributed to a wide array of gods. Artifacts dating to a time before recorded history suggest that the religion of the distant past reflected this world, consisting mainly of rituals devised to influence events under the control of these gods.

The steady advancement of human societies brought about changes in religion as in all other things. Through time, religion came to be seen as a system of beliefs and practices that gave meaning to—or allowed acceptance of—anything that transcended the natural or the known. And, the belief in many gods ultimately was replaced in many cultures by the belief in a Supreme Being.

As in the distant past, however, religion still provides answers to timeless questions: How, why, and by whom was the universe created? What is the ultimate meaning of human life? Why is life inevitably followed by death? Does the human soul continue to exist after death, and if so, in what form? Why is there pain and suffering in the world, and why is there evil?

In addition, all the major world religions provide their followers with a concrete and clearly stated ethical code. They offer a set of moral instructions, defining virtue and evil and what is required to achieve goodness. One of these universal moral codes is compassion toward others above all else. Thus, Judaism, Christianity, Islam, Hinduism, Buddhism, Confucianism, and Taoism each teach a version of the so-called golden rule, or in the words of Jesus Christ, "As ye would that men should do to you, do ye also to them likewise." (Luke 6:31) For example, Confucius instructed his disciples to "never impose on others what you would not choose for yourself." (*Analects:* 12:2) The Hindu epic poem, Mahabharata, identifies the core of all Hindu teaching as not doing unto others what you do not wish done to yourself. Similarly Muhammad declared that no Muslim could be a true believer unless he desired for his brother no less than that which he desires for himself.

It is ironic, then, that although compassionate concern for others forms the heart of all the major religions' moral teachings, religion has also been at the root of countless conflicts throughout history. It has been suggested that much of the appeal that religions hold for humankind lies in their unswerving faith in the truth of their particular vision. Throughout history, most religions have shared a profound confidence that their interpretation of life, God, and the universe is the right one, thus giving their followers a sense of certainty in an uncertain and often fragile existence. Given the assurance displayed by most religions regarding the fundamental correctness of their teachings and practices, it is perhaps not surprising that religious intolerance has fueled disputes and even full-scale wars between peoples and nations time and time again, from the Crusades of medieval times to the current bloodshed in Northern Ireland and the Middle East.

Today, as violent religious conflicts trouble many parts of our world, it has become more important than ever to learn about the similarities as well as the differences between faiths. One of the most effective ways to accomplish this is by examining the beliefs, customs, and values of various religions. In the Religions of the World series, students will find a clear description of the core creeds, rituals, ethical teachings, and sacred texts of the world's major religions. In-depth explorations of how these faiths changed over time, how they have influenced the social customs, laws, and education of the countries in which they are practiced, and the particular challenges each one faces in coming years are also featured.

Extensive quotations from primary source materials, especially the core scriptures of each faith, and a generous number of secondary source quotations from the works of respected modern scholars are included in each volume in the series. It is hoped that by gaining insight into the faiths of other peoples and nations, students will not only gain a deeper appreciation and respect for different religious beliefs and practices, but will also gain new perspectives on and understanding of their own religious traditions.

A Growing Religion

More than 300 million people throughout the world practice Buddhism, a religion established by Siddhārtha Gautama—known as the Buddha—in India during the sixth century B.C. From India, Buddhism spread throughout Asia, and today it is a major religion in Japan, Tibet, Laos, Myanmar, Sri Lanka, Taiwan, Singapore, Thailand, Cambodia, Bhutan, and Vietnam. Although the People's Republic of China has officially declared itself an atheist country, Buddhism is also practiced by many Chinese.

Buddhism is practiced in Western countries as well. In fact, in recent years it has become particularly popular in the United States, where the number of people converting to Buddhism from some other religion is growing. Sociologists estimate that approximately 1 million Americans who grew up Christian or Jewish are now practicing some form of Buddhism. The readership of *Tricycle*, a New York–based magazine for Americans interested in Buddhism, has grown from five thousand in 1991 to sixty-five thousand in 2001. In addition, as of 2001 there were 1,166 English-language Buddhist teaching centers across the country.

Individuality and Personal Responsibility
One of the main reasons for Buddhism's popularity is its acceptance of individuality. Buddhists do not persecute non-

Buddhists, nor do they argue that there is only one right way to practice Buddhism. In fact, Buddhists believe that the essence of the Buddha's teachings is that each person should make his or her own decisions regarding how Buddhism should be practiced. Consequently, many different forms of Buddhism have developed over the centuries, and Buddhists are generally accepting of all of these variations. Tibetan Buddhist nun Thubten Chodron expresses the common Buddhist view of Buddhism's doctrinal variety:

The fact that there are a variety of practices within the Buddhist doctrine attests to the Buddha's skill in guiding people according to their dispositions and needs. It is extremely important . . . to have respect for all the traditions and their practitioners. Since the teaching of all these traditions originate from the Buddha, if we disparage one tradition, we are disparaging the Buddha and his teachings.[1]

This level of acceptance stems from a central feature of Buddhist

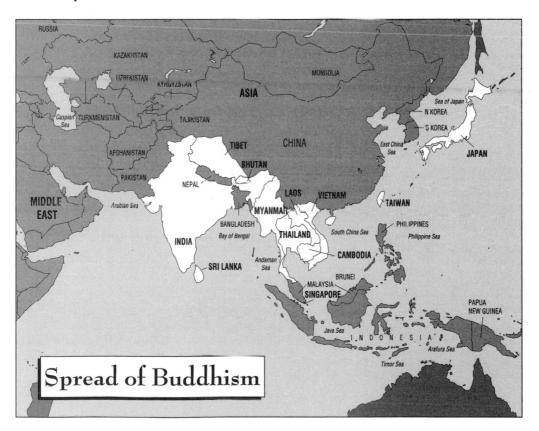

Spread of Buddhism

teachings: A person should find spirituality within, through introspection and careful thought, rather than unthinkingly accept religious dogma that has been imposed by others. In general, Buddhists believe that people should look inward to better themselves rather than relying on someone else—whether a religious leader, a church, or a deity—to give them a better life. Buddhists are responsible for their own knowledge, awareness, and contentment, and many converts to Buddhism say that they find this emphasis on personal responsibility empowering. American Buddhist Steve Hagan stresses this approach to Buddhism in his book *Buddhism Plain and Simple*, in which he says,

> Buddhism is not a belief system. It's not about accepting certain tenets or believing a set of claims or principles. In fact, it's quite the opposite. It's about examining the world clearly and carefully, about testing everything and every idea. . . . Not least of all, . . . we must examine the Buddha's teaching itself. The Buddha himself invited people on all occasions to test him. "Don't believe me because you see me as your teacher," he said. "Don't believe in me because others do. And don't believe anything because you've read it in a book, either. Don't put your faith in reports, or tradition, or hearsay, or the authority of religious leaders or texts. . . . Know for yourselves that certain things are unwholesome and wrong. And when you do, then give them up. And when you know for yourselves that certain things are wholesome and good, then accept them and follow them."[2]

Living in the Moment

As part of the process of attaining self-knowledge, Buddhism promotes cooperation, nonviolence, and other positive ways of relating to people. In addition, it emphasizes the importance of remaining calm and centered by means of meditation and changes in attitude. Many adherents of other faiths are attracted to this aspect of Buddhism, thinking that they too might achieve inner calm without necessarily embracing Buddhism as a religion. To this end, there are many Christians and Jews who practice Buddhist meditation techniques while remaining committed to their own faith.

The Buddha also taught that life should be experienced in the moment, and this notion has particular appeal in modern times, when people often feel compelled to rush ahead to the next phase of life. In discussing this appeal, Buddhist Chögyam Trungpa Rinpoche said,

> Usually, the basic thread that runs through our experience is our desire to have a purely goal-oriented process: everything, we feel, should be done in relation to our ambition, our competitiveness, our one-upmanship. . . . [Buddhism] . . . cuts through this small, goal-oriented vision, so that everything becomes purely a learning process. This permits us to relate with our lives fully and properly. . . . This aspect [of Buddhism] . . . is particularly applicable in America, where it is quite fashionable to blame everything on others and to feel that all kinds of elements in one's relationships or surroundings are unhealthy or polluted. . . . [Practicing Buddhism] means that all of life is regarded as a fertile situation and a learning situation, always. Whatever occurs—pain or pleasure, good or bad, justice or injustice—is part of the learning process.[3]

This view of life as a learning process fosters a tolerance and adaptability that has served Buddhism well over many centuries. At various times, Buddhism has appeared destined to wither into obscurity, only to experience a resurgence that attracted many new followers. Such a resurgence is currently taking place today. It is likely that Buddhism will continue to thrive in the future, perhaps adding still more new traditions in accordance with changing cultures.

chapter one

The Origins of Buddhism

Buddhism began with one man, Siddhārtha Gautama of India. However, in developing the tenets of his religion, he was influenced by the prevailing beliefs of his time. The story of Buddhism, therefore, begins with Hinduism.

The Vedic Age

In ancient times, most of India's population was concentrated in two river basins, the River Indus basin and the Ganges River basin. From around 3000 B.C. to 1500 B.C., the River Indus basin (which is now within Pakistan) was the site of an advanced civilization known today as the Indus Valley Culture. By 1500 B.C., the buildings of its great cities were crumbling and its people were scattered throughout the valley. (Historians do not know why the River Indus culture disappeared, but some theorize that it was destroyed by internal conflict.) When a group of nomadic warriors known as the Aryans invaded the region from the northwest, they conquered it easily. Their beliefs then mingled with those of the existing populace, a process that created the religion of Hinduism. This religion soon spread to the Ganges River basin.

Historians call the period when the new culture established by the Aryan invasion dominated India—from around 1500 B.C. to 500 B.C.—the Vedic Age. This name, from the ancient Indian word *veda*, or knowledge, comes from the Vedas, the oldest Hindu scriptures. Originally passed on orally, the Vedas were eventually written down in a series of works: the Rigveda, the Samaveda, the Yajurveda, and the Atharvaveda.

From Hindu scriptures, it is clear that although the ancient Indians worshiped many gods and goddesses, they eventually came to believe that all of these deities were part of one universal spirit, the Brahman. There are many manifestations of the Brahman, including Brahmā, the creator of the universe; Vishnu, the preserver of the universe; Shiva, who has the power to destroy the universe; and Shiva's wife Kali (also known as Durga, Parvati, or Uma), who is both the goddess of destruction and the goddess of new life and motherhood. Many Hindus consider Kali to be the symbol of a cycle of life that moves from birth to death to rebirth.

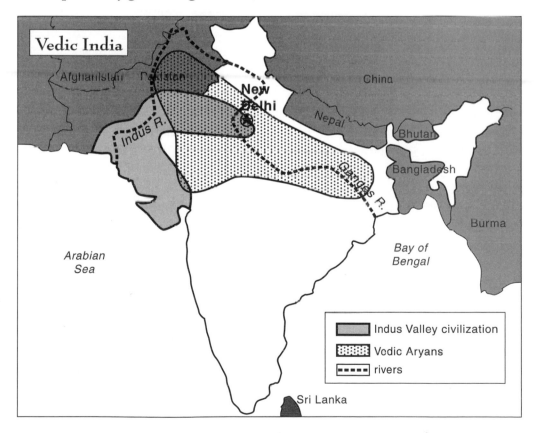

Vedic India

Afghanistan — Pakistan — New Delhi — China — Nepal — Bhutan — Bangladesh — Burma

Indus R. — Ganges R.

Arabian Sea

Bay of Bengal

Sri Lanka

Indus Valley civilization
Vedic Aryans
rivers

Five–headed Brahma, the creator of the universe according to Hindu beliefs, sits on his Vahana, the cosmic goose.

Reincarnation

This concept of rebirth figured prominently in the Indian beliefs at the time. During the Vedic Age, various theories developed regarding what exactly happened to the soul after death. Gradually, the prevailing idea came to be that, after the death of a person's physical body, the person's soul would take residence in the body of another creature, one just being born. In this way, a person would live not just one life but a series of lives, one after the other.

Some people believed that this process of rebirth after death, which is called reincarnation or samsara, would never place a human soul in an animal body; others, however, believed that a person might spend one lifetime as a human and the next as a lower life-

form, perhaps even a worm. In either case, whatever happened in one life was believed to influence the next reincarnation. Under this concept, which is known as the law of karma, some ancient Indians believed that the soul of a person who behaved badly might, after death, move down to the level of a worm, while an animal that lived a good life might live its next life as a human. Indians who believed that a human could be reborn only as another human thought that reincarnation provided a person with the chance to better his or her status in life.

This opportunity for betterment was particularly important because of the hereditary, hierarchical caste system that developed during the Vedic Age. This system dictated that a person was born into a certain caste, or social group, and could associate only with other members of that group. The castes, in order of prestige, were the priesthood (the *brahmana*); the warriors and aristocrats (the *kshatriyas*); the traders, merchants, and professional workers (the *vaishyas*); and the agricultural workers (the *shudras*). (In later centuries, the Indians would add another caste, the Untouchables, for people deemed unworthy to be in any of the other castes.)

Under the caste system, people were doomed to remain within the social group into which they had been born.

No one could ever move out of that caste, whether to a higher or lower one, or even associate with someone from another caste. Through reincarnation, however, a person could hope to move to a higher caste during his or her next lifetime—provided the person lived a good enough life.

Spiritual Enlightenment

Initially, ancient Hindus defined a good life as one that was lived in

The Buddhist Cosmos

Buddhists have a highly complex view of the cosmos. They believe that the universe is made up of not just one world but many worlds, each with its own gods. Buddhists disagree on just how many worlds there are. However, Buddhist texts typically refer to a "thousandfold world-system," a "twice-thousandfold world-system," or a "thrice-thousandfold world-system." A being might be reborn into any one of these worlds, and into any one of thirty-one realms of existence within each world. Rupert Gethin, in his book The Foundations of Buddhism, *describes this system.*

It is the lower levels of the universe, that is the world of the five senses, that arrange themselves into the various distinct 'world-spheres' or Cakravādas. At the centre of a cakra-vāda is the great world mountain, Meru or Sineru. This is surrounded by seven concentric rings of mountains and seas. Beyond these mountains, in the four cardinal directions, are four continents. The southern continent, Jambudvīpa or 'the continent of the rose-apple tree', is the continent inhabited by ordinary human beings; the southern part, below the towering abode of snows (himālaya) is effectively India, the land where buddhas arise. In the spaces between world-spheres and below are various hells, while in the shadow of the slopes of Mount Meru dwell the jealous gods called Asuras. . . . On the slopes of Mount Meru itself and rising above its peak are the six realms inhabited by the gods of the sense-sphere. A great Brahmā of the lower realms of pure form may rule over a thousand such world-spheres, while Brahmās of the higher realms of the form sphere are said to rule over a hundred thousand. . . . In general, . . . rebirth in the lower realms is considered to be the result of relatively . . . bad karma, while rebirth in the higher realms the result of relatively . . . good karma. Correspondingly, the lower the realm, the more unpleasant and unhappy one's condition; the higher the realm the more pleasant, happy, and refined one's condition.

accordance with dharma, a concept that involves an adherence to laws, social and moral obligations, and religious duties. Eventually, though, some people began to think that some kind of spiritual awakening or enlightenment was also required before a person could move up to a better life through reincarnation.

During the Vedic Age, members of the priesthood sought this kind of enlightenment, believing that it would give them the power to control the cosmos. Specifically, they thought that if they could understand the true nature of the universe, known as the Ultimate Reality or Brahman, and perform rituals in accordance with this understanding, they would be able to influence events on earth. They also believed that understanding the true nature of the human soul, or atman, would allow them to control reincarnation.

As the Vedic Age progressed, warriors and aristocrats increasingly sought this type of spiritual enlightenment as well. Some believed, like the priests, that it would give them control over the cosmos. Others felt that spiritual enlightenment would bring them so much perfection that their souls would no longer be reincarnated but would instead reside within the Ultimate Reality, among the gods. To this end, many young men abandoned their families to live a spartan life alone in forests or on mountaintops, believing that the solitude of these places would help them with their inward journey toward enlightenment. Such individuals were called ascetics.

As more and more people became ascetics, India's priests felt threatened, particularly since many ascetics seemed more holy than they were. As a result, the priests spoke out against the ascetic lifestyle, arguing that it went against the purpose of youth, which was to be engaged in the world; only old men, the priests argued, should undertake the life of an ascetic. Other critics accused the ascetics of being selfish for abandoning their responsibilities and called them useless to Indian society.

However, many ascetics felt that they were doing something important for society as well as for themselves. In achieving enlightenment, they hoped to find a way to better the human condition. Most Indians suffered a great deal in their lifetimes; poverty and its attendant misery were widespread. Yet because of its caste system, Indian society did not generally allow individuals to improve their circumstances. Consequently, ascetics thought that the spiritual realm might offer all Indians what the ordinary realm did not: a chance at happiness.

Ascetics disagreed, though, on just how this chance might best be obtained. By the late sixth century B.C., several different approaches to asceticism had developed, each offering its own beliefs on how to attain enlightenment, if indeed such attainment was possible. (Some ascetics believed that the best a person could hope to achieve was peace of mind rather than a truly enlightened state.) One of these approaches was Buddhism, which involved complex ideas about how a person had to behave in order to achieve spiritual enlightenment. Established by Siddhārtha Gautama, who called himself the Buddha, or "enlightened one," Buddhism reflected its founder's unique revelations about reincarnation and the Ultimate Reality and their relationship to human suffering.

Born the Buddha

There are many stories about Siddhārtha's path to enlightenment, and historians have gone to the earliest sources in an attempt to separate fact from legend. These sources include one of the earliest biographies of the Buddha, the *Buddhacarita (Acts of the Buddha)* by first- or second-century

As part of his inward journey toward enlightenment, a Hindu ascetic meditates beneath a Bodhi tree.

Indian poet Ashvaghosa. Ashvaghosa drew on oral histories of the Buddha that had been passed down for hundreds of years after the Buddha's death. Until the poet's work, the only written record of the Buddha's existence were stone monuments erected in India 250 years after his death. Historians accept these inscribed pillars, located at various sites that hold significance to the Buddha's life and teaching, as evidence that Siddhārtha Gautama truly existed and was not simply a mythical figure.

From the earliest writings about the Buddha, modern scholars have determined that Siddhārtha Gautama was born around 563 B.C. on the northern edge of the Ganges River basin, an area that is now part of Nepal. Gautama was his clan name, and his father, Shuddhodana, was most likely a king, or at least an aristocrat and prominent political leader of a people called the Shakyas. Siddhārtha's mother, Mahamaya, died only a week after giving birth to him, so he was raised by her sister, Mahapajapati, who was probably another of Shuddhodana's wives. (At that time and place, a man could have many wives, and the more prominent a man, the more wives he had.)

There are many stories about the Buddha's birth, and most of them suggest that people knew he was spe-

cial from the beginning. In one story, Mahamaya had a dream the night she conceived her son in which a white elephant (an animal sacred to the Indian people) entered her womb and became the Buddha-to-be, or bodhisattva. In another story, the Buddha was born from Mahamaya's side, without blood, and water rained on the mother and child from above to cleanse and purify them. According to E. J. Thomas in his book *The Life of the Buddha,*

> As soon as he is born, the Bodhisattva . . . firmly standing with even feet goes firmly to the north with seven long steps, a white parasol being held over him (by the gods). He surveys all the quarters, and in a lordly voice says, "I am the chief in the world, I am the best in the world, I am the first in the world. This is my last birth. There is now no existence again.[4]

In other words, the Buddha knew from birth that he would achieve perfection and therefore his soul would not need another reincarnation. Other people supposedly knew this as well. A wise man who saw the infant after birth was said to have noted thirty-two marks on the boy's body which indicated that he would grow up not only to achieve enlightenment but also to be a

Siddhārtha Gautama, the first Buddha, was destined from birth to confront demons, such as the one pictured here.

great teacher and spiritual leader. In another story, a wise man who heard about Mahamaya's dream was said to have proclaimed that it meant Siddhārtha would grow up to be either a great king or a famous ascetic.

His Father's Influence

The idea that Siddhārtha was destined to take up a life of spiritual pursuit upset his father, because it meant that the boy would one day abandon his duties as heir. To prevent this, Shuddhodana became determined to keep Siddhārtha away from spiritual influences. Moreover, since Shuddhodana believed that many people turned to religion as an antidote to the hardships of life, he ensured that Siddhārtha's life was as pleasant as possible. In fact, he ordered that his son should never see anything ugly or painful. This meant that whenever the boy traveled from one of Shuddhodana's palaces to another, servants went ahead of his chariot to make sure that nothing unpleasant was visible along the way. When he was not traveling, Siddhārtha was always confined within palace walls, where he ate the best food, wore the most luxurious clothes, and had many servants and beautiful women to provide him with anything he wanted.

This lifestyle continued even after Siddhārtha married his cousin Yashodhara when he was just sixteen years old. About thirteen years later, the couple had a son, and the family continued to live in the palace under Shuddhodana's supervision. Shortly before his son was born, however, Siddhārtha became restless. According to some stories, he begged his father to allow him to see some of the outside world, and his father relented. According to other accounts, Siddhārtha sneaked out of the palace without his father's permission.

In either case, driven in a chariot by his groom Channa, Siddhārtha went out four times. On the first outing he saw an old man, on the second a man with a disfiguring disease, on the third a corpse being carried on a litter, and on the fourth a wandering holy man. The first three outings were traumatic for Siddhārtha, who had never before been confronted with the ravages of time and sickness. Suddenly he realized that life was fleeting, and all of his comforts seemed meaningless. But when Siddhārtha encountered the holy man, he felt a sense of peace because the man radiated contentment. As a result, Siddhārtha began to think that spiritual pursuits might offer a release from worldly suffering.

Siddhārtha was further confronted with such suffering when, shortly after his four outings, he was sent to observe farming techniques on his father's land. Shuddhodana thought this visit would imbue his son with a sense of his position and responsibility in society. Instead, the experience repulsed Siddhārtha, who witnessed firsthand the poverty and filth in which the workers lived and the cruelty with which they treated their oxen. Now more than ever, Siddhārtha longed to leave his father's world. In fact, when Siddhārtha's son was born, he named him Rahula, or "fetter," because he viewed the boy as a burden that kept him imprisoned in his present life.

Abandoning the Palace

One night shortly after his son's birth, Siddhārtha exchanged his luxurious clothes for the yellow robe of a holy man, shaved off his hair and beard, and sneaked out of the palace empty-handed. For months he wandered throughout northeast India, begging for food and sleeping on hard ground in the hope that a life of self-denial would bring him to enlightenment.

Specifically, he wanted to gain insights into human suffering, to understand why people suffer and how spirituality might lead to an end to that suffering.

During his travels, Siddhārtha encountered first one holy man and then another, who taught him meditation techniques and schooled him in Hindu beliefs. Finally, Siddhārtha settled near the banks of the Nairañjanā River. By this time, he had decided that enlightenment was eluding him because he was not suffering enough. He started sleeping on thorns and routinely held his breath until he experienced pain, which was followed by unconsciousness. He also began to fast intermittently, never eating enough to sustain his health, and his body grew emaciated. Siddhārtha later said of this time:

> All my limbs became like the knotted joints of withered creepers, my

Preparing to search for enlightenment, Siddhārtha shaves off his hair and beard.

buttocks like a bullock's hoof, my protruding backbone like a string of balls, my gaunt ribs like the crazy rafters of a tumble-down shed. My eyes lay deep in their sockets, their pupils sparkling like water in a deep well. As an unripe gourd shrivels and shrinks in a hot wind, so became my scalp. If I thought, "I will touch the skin of my belly," it was the skin of my backbone that I also took hold of, since the skin of my belly and back met. The hairs, rotting at the roots, fell away from my body when I stroked my limbs.[5]

Word of Siddhārtha's dramatic quest for enlightenment spread, and soon he attracted five ascetics as followers. When Siddhārtha became too weak to look after himself, these men helped him. This went on for six years, until finally Siddhārtha realized that weakening the body was no way to enlighten the mind. He began eating regular meals again; his five followers, believing that Siddhārtha had given up his quest for enlightenment, abandoned him.

The Enlightenment

Shortly thereafter, on his thirty-fifth birthday, Siddhārtha went to the river to bathe. There he met a woman who gave him rice boiled in cream and sweetened with wild honey, the most pleasurable food he had eaten since his quest for enlightenment began. According to scholar John Snelling in his book *The Buddhist Handbook*, this experience presented Siddhārtha with a new thought:

> There was one thing that he had not really tried [during his quest]—a middle way between the luxurious and the ascetic ways. He also recalled an incident during a ploughing festival when as a child he had sat beneath the rose-apple tree and entered a state of meditation. He thought: "Might that be the way to Enlightenment?"[6]

With this question in mind, Siddhārtha sat beneath the branches of a ficus tree on a cushion of grass, determined to remain there until enlightenment came. According to Buddhist scriptures, at this moment an evil god, Mara, saw what Siddhārtha was doing and grew upset, because he did not want any mortal to learn how to end suffering. In response, he tried to destroy Siddhārtha's sense of purpose, challenging Siddhārtha's worthiness to seek enlightenment, criticizing the man's decision to leave his family, and send-

Determined to achieve enlightenment, Siddhārtha meditates despite the efforts of demons to torture him with thirst, lust, and other distractions.

ing an army of demons to torment Siddhārtha with thirst, lust, and other earthly discomforts and distractions. Siddhārtha, however, remained strong against these assaults, continuing to meditate under the tree.

John Snelling says that although this story is probably a myth, it offers true insights into what Siddhārtha must have been going through as he searched for spiritual enlightenment. Snelling explains:

We might interpret [stories of Mara's attacks on the Buddha] to

mean that there were times during Siddhārtha's quest when he was tempted to give up. He may occasionally have felt that he had done enough and should go home and discharge his social duty. At other times perhaps powerful fears rose up within him. He may have become worried that he might go mad, that what he was doing might project him into some outlandish psychic state. Fear of the supernatural may also have hit him, or fear of death, or even an *angst* more frightful than that of death: a kind of existential terror of utter annihilation or non-being. We can take it, however, that he did not succumb to any of these.[7]

Instead, through deeper and deeper states of meditation, Siddhārtha gradually gained knowledge that brought him to a place of spiritual enlightenment, whereupon he began calling himself the Buddha, the "enlightened one." What the Buddha learned, however, is beyond description. The reason for this becomes obvious when one considers how difficult it was for the Buddha to obtain the knowledge.

As Andrew Skilton explains in his book *A Concise History of Buddhism*,

There are many accounts and formulas which describe the nature of Buddhist insight, yet ultimately they fall short of the experience itself—otherwise one could become Enlightened merely by reading a book or listening to an exposition of [Buddhist teachings].[8]

Generally, though, these accounts agree that Siddhārtha received certain insights into the true nature of

A temple in Bihar, India, was constructed next to the bodhi tree where Buddha attained enlightenment.

the world, karma, and reincarnation. He saw that the cycle of birth and rebirth was always linked to human suffering, and he saw how to end that cycle. He also achieved nirvana, which Buddhists define as an entry into another mode of existence, and understood how to teach others to do the same by overcoming desire, hatred, and delusion.

Having realized all this, Siddhārtha became the Buddha, and later the tree beneath which he attained enlightenment became known as the Bodhi (enlightenment) tree. The Buddha remained under this tree for a while after receiving enlightenment in order to meditate further. (The amount of time he remained there was seven days in some accounts, four or seven weeks in others.) He then set out to teach people what he had discovered. According to some stories, the Buddha doubted whether anyone would understand his teachings, but the god Brahmā assured him that there were at least a few people capable of learning them. So the Buddha began preaching sermons, and his teachings soon took hold in India.

chapter | two

The Teachings of the Buddha

The Buddha wrote no books on his teachings, nor in all likelihood did his disciples. For more than four hundred years, both during and after the Buddha's lifetime, his words—or sutras—were passed on orally rather than in writing. Sometimes these words were forgotten or changed, usually by people who did not fully understand them, and when some monks in Sri Lanka finally decided to write them down (on palm leaves), only one monk could recite the Buddha's entire teachings from memory. According to Buddhist stories, the monk was quite arrogant about this accomplishment. Vietnamese Buddhist monk Thich Nhat Hanh says, "When we hear this, we feel a little uneasy knowing that an arrogant monk may not have been the best vehicle to transmit the teachings of the Buddha."[9]

Moreover, by the time the idea of writing down the Buddha's teachings took hold, there were already many different traditions, or schools, of Buddhism, and each expressed the Buddha's teachings in different ways. Therefore, according to Thich Nhat Hanh,

Often, we need to study several discourses and compare them in order to understand which is the true teaching of the Buddha. It is like stringing precious jewels together to make a necklace. If we see each sūtra in light of the overall body of teachings, we will not be attached to any one teaching. With comparative study and looking deeply into the meaning of the texts, we can surmise what is a solid teaching that will help our practice and what is probably an incorrect transmission.[10]

In this way, scholars have been able to distill the essence of the Buddha's teachings and know about the sermons he delivered during his lifetime.

Samsara

The Buddha sought out the five ascetics who had earlier abandoned him during his quest for enlightenment and delivered his first sermon to them in the town of Isipatana (now Sarnath), India, where he found them in a park established as a deer refuge. Because of the location, many Buddhists call the Buddha's first sermon the Deer Park Sermon.

The Buddha began this sermon by sprinkling a handful of rice grains on the ground to outline a circle. He explained that this circle was the wheel of life, which continues cycling through existence after existence so that every sentient being experiences birth, life, decay, death, and rebirth over and over again. The Buddha called this process samsara, or "wandering," because through repeated rebirth a being wanders from one realm of existence to another, always

Buddha's sūtras were later translated and written down by monks to accurately preserve his teachings.

This sculpture represents the Buddha's first sermon, the Deer Park Sermon, in which he described the wheel of life, which is a continual cycle through existence.

searching for permanent happiness and security that can never be found in an impermanent universe. The Buddha suggested that the way to end samsara was to become a buddha—an "enlightened one" like himself—by gaining certain profound insights into the human condition. Buddhas, he said, would not be reborn but instead, after death, would attain transcendence, a state apart from the cycle of birth-death-birth. Later in life, he explained the separateness of a buddha:

Just as a blue, red, or white lotus, born in water and grown up in water, having risen above the water stands unstained by water, even so do I, born in the world and grown up in the world, having overcome the world, dwell unstained by the world. Understand that I am a buddha.[11]

As he continued his Deer Park Sermon, the Buddha recounted his own journey to enlightenment, pointing out that neither his life of pleasure nor his life of asceticism brought him to his goal. Instead, he found enlightenment through what he called the middle way, which avoids both extremes by satisfying the needs of the body and mind without going to excess. He advocated that other people follow his example; he also provided many details about how people should live their lives if they wanted to end samsara.

The First Noble Truth

Buddhists sometimes refer to the Deer Park Sermon as "Setting in Motion the Wheel of the Doctrine," because in it the Buddha presented the cornerstones of Buddhist doctrine—specifically, the concepts of the Four Noble Truths and the Eightfold Path. The truths reflect the Buddha's understanding of why humans suffer, and the Eightfold Path was his way out of suffering. Together, these concepts make up the dharma, the essence of Buddhist teachings, which defines the "right" way to behave.

The first noble truth is suffering, or *dukkha*. The word *dukkha* comes from a Sanskrit word meaning an unbalanced wheel, and the kind of physical and mental suffering to which it refers in Buddhism is a constant condition rather than an intermittent pain. Steve Hagan, in his book *Buddhism Plain and Simple*, explains:

> In the Buddha's time the . . . image may have been of a cart with an out-of-true wheel being pulled along. You can imagine how uncomfortable it must feel to ride in such a vehicle. The repeated wobble, rise, and drop starts out as annoying, then becomes steadily more distracting and disturbing. Maybe there's a little pleasure in it for the rider at first—a little bounce, perhaps—but after a while it becomes more and more vexing. . . . Something basic and important isn't right. It bothers us, makes us unhappy, time after time. With each turn of the wheel, each passing day, we experience pain.[12]

The Buddha himself identified all aspects of the human condition on earth as involving suffering, which at its heart is the attempt to hold on to something. In describing his first noble truth, he said,

> What now is the noble truth of suffering? Birth is suffering; decay is suffering; death is suffering; sorrow, lamentation, pain, grief, and despair are suffering; not to

get what one wants is suffering; in short, the five aggregates of clinging are suffering.[13]

By the "aggregates of clinging," the Buddha was referring to those aspects of existence that tie people to the material as opposed to the spiritual world. He noted that everything material is impermanent, subject to decay and loss, and he argued that only unhappiness could come from such things.

Understanding Suffering

To disciples seeking enlightenment, for each noble truth the Buddha assigned a task to be mastered. For the first noble truth, the task was to fully understand human suffering. Achieving this understanding is not as easy as it might sound. For cen-

This shrine in the town of Sarnath, India, marks the spot where the Buddha delivered the Deer Park Sermon, in which he described the Four Noble Truths and the Eightfold Path.

turies, Buddhists have disagreed on what the Buddha meant when he spoke about the nature of suffering. Thich Nhat Hanh addresses this controversy in his book *The Heart of the Buddha's Teachings*:

> If we are not careful in the way we practice [Buddhism], we may have the tendency to make the words of our teacher into a doctrine or an ideology. Since the Buddha said that the First Noble Truth is suffering, many good students of the Buddha have used their skills to prove that everything on Earth is suffering. . . . Whatever comes together eventually has to come apart; therefore all composite things are described as suffering. Even things that have not yet decayed, such as mountains, rivers, and the sun, are seen to be suffering, because they will decay and cause suffering eventually. When you believe that everything composed is suffering, how can you find joy?[14]

Hanh argues that the Buddha did not mean to suggest that objects such as tables and chairs experience suffering. However, other Buddhists disagree, saying that as the Buddha explained the concept, everything subject to decay or loss is indeed suffering.

The Second, Third, and Fourth Noble Truths

Buddhists have also disagreed about the Buddha's second noble truth, which addresses the cause of suffering. The Buddha identified this cause as craving and all attempts to satisfy craving, which was defined as a desire for possessions, pleasures, and experiences. The Buddha said,

> What now is the noble truth of the origin of suffering? It is craving, which gives rise to repeated existence, is bound up with pleasure and lust, and always seeks fresh enjoyment here and there; that is, sensual craving, craving for existence and craving for the nonexistence.[15]

The third noble truth is that suffering will end if and when craving ends. On this subject, the Buddha said,

> What now is the noble truth of the cessation of suffering? It is the complete fading away and cessation of craving, its forsaking and abandonment, liberation and detachment from it.[16]

Some Buddhists believe that the Buddha saw craving as the only cause of suffering. Others believe that he

The First Words of an Enlightened Buddha

In an essay titled "The Life of the Buddha," which appears in An Introduction to the Buddha and His Teachings, *co-editor Sherab Chödzin Kohn says that the Buddha told his followers that when he attained complete Enlightenment, the first words that came to him were the following:*

Seeking but not finding the House Builder,

I traveled through the round of countless births:

O painful is birth ever and again.

    House builder, you have now been seen;

    You shall not build the house again.

    Your rafters have been broken down;

    Your ridge pole is demolished too.

My mind has now attained the unformed nirvana

And reached the end of every kind of craving.

saw other causes as well, even if he did not name them. For example, Thich Nhat Hanh says,

[A] common misunderstanding of the Buddha's teaching is that all of our suffering is caused by craving. In the *Discourse on Turning the Wheel of the Dharma*, the Buddha did say that craving is the cause of suffering, but he said this because craving is the first on the list of afflictions (*kleshas*). If we use our intelligence, we can see that craving can be a cause of pain, but other afflictions such as anger, igno-rance, suspicion, arrogance, and wrong views can also cause pain and suffering. Ignorance, which gives rise to wrong perceptions, is responsible for much of our pain. To make the sutras shorter and therefore easier to memorize, the first item on a list was often used to represent the whole list. . . . To say that craving is the cause of all our suffering is too simplistic.[17]

The tasks associated with the sec-ond and third noble truths are to identify one's own cravings and to realize that nirvana, an exalted state of enlightenment, offers a deliverance from suffering. The task of the fourth noble truth is more complex. In this truth, the Buddha taught that the way to end craving is to act and think in ways known collectively as the Noble Eightfold Path, or more simply the Eightfold Path; following this path might ultimately enable a person to reach nirvana. The task associated with the fourth noble truth is to develop all eight aspects of the Eightfold Path in order to reach nirvana.

The Eightfold Path

The components of the Eightfold Path are typically presented to students of Buddhism as a numbered list, but they must actually be developed concurrently rather than consecutively. The components are as follows:

1. Right Understanding
2. Right Thought
3. Right Speech
4. Right Action
5. Right Livelihood
6. Right Effort
7. Right Mindfulness
8. Right Concentration

The first two factors relate to wisdom, or *prajñā*. Right Understanding means learning the Buddha's teachings and developing a full understanding of them, not only by thinking about them but by testing their wisdom against experience. Right Thought means developing the motivation to practice Buddhism and to experience selflessness, in part by becoming more concerned with others than with oneself.

The next three factors relate to morality, or *shila*. Right Speech means always speaking the truth and never gossiping, backbiting, swearing, or otherwise using speech in a harmful manner. Right Action means behaving decently—specifically, by not killing, displaying cruelty, stealing, or overindulging in activities related to the senses. The latter includes overeating, abusing the body with drugs and/or alcohol, and spending so much time on intellectual pursuits that other important aspects of life are ignored. Right Livelihood means earning a living through ways that do not harm living things or the environment or compromise one's integrity.

The last three factors relate to concentration, or *samadhi*. Right Effort means regulating one's energy so that the proper amount of effort is put into each endeavor; overzealousness is to be avoided as much as laziness. Right Mindfulness means becoming aware of the body and the mind, both to prepare for meditation and to cultivate self-awareness and see the world as it really is. Finally, Right Concentration means achieving deep meditation, through which one might find enlightenment as the Buddha did.

Buddhist Meditation

In subsequent sermons at the deer park and elsewhere, the Buddha was specific in his advice regarding meditation. At heart, meditation has two aspects, Shamatha ("calm abiding") and Vipashyana (insight). In Shamatha, the practitioner concentrates solely on one thing, either internal or external (one's breathing, for example, or a colored object), that does not evoke any emotion. As the period of concentration progresses, the mind should become calmer and calmer. Once a certain level of calm is reached, the practitioner is ready for Vipashyana, a heightened sense of awareness when the mind can observe and analyze whatever comes to its attention. The Buddha taught that, while in this state, one can learn many truths.

Learning to practice Buddhist meditation takes time and can be difficult. John Snelling, in his book *The Buddhist Handbook*, reports that this difficulty stems from two particular areas of concern: mental focus and a preoccupation with results rather than process. He explains:

Things rarely go swimmingly in meditation, especially at first. Attention slips and the mind wanders away on beguiling trains of thought and fantasy. When this happens, the fact should be noted and the attention returned to the object of concentration. It will probably have to be brought back time and time and time again. The most important thing is not to set ambitious goals or strive for results—that is more likely to frustrate rather than hasten the development of concentration—but to simply perform the practice patiently and aim first and foremost at remaining aware of what is going on in the now. Sometimes the mind is in turmoil throughout a meditation session and cannot develop any degree of concentration; the practice then is to remain fully mindful of this.[18]

The Buddha also viewed meditation as a way to weaken the "I"—the ego or self. He believed that each person's "I" stood in the way of inner peace and that in order to find such peace it was necessary to behave and think in certain ways that would bring freedom from ego. Only after "forgetting oneself," as Buddhists refer to this freedom, could a person reach nirvāna, an exalted state of enlightenment or spirituality. As part of forgetting oneself, the Buddha advocated a concern for others above self. In addition, he considered judgmentalism to be a manifestation of the ego, and therefore urged people not to judge or criticize the beliefs and practices of others.

Criticizing Hindu Practices

However, the Buddha did suggest that some of the practices of Hinduism would hinder a person's journey toward enlightenment. Specifically, although he incorporated the traditional concept of karma into his teachings, suggesting that the behaviors of one life will affect the conditions of the

A Buddhist monk practices deep meditation, a vital element in the effort to attain enlightenment.

next, he rejected the Hindu concept of the soul, or atman. The Buddha insisted that, although there was rebirth, there was no reincarnation, because reincarnation involves the transmission of a relatively unchanging consciousness (in other words, the soul) from one body to another. Instead, the Buddha believed that a person is made up of feelings, perceptions, ideas, and other elements that are constantly changing, and when these elements are reborn, they are not the same as when they previously came together in life.

In explaining this concept, the Buddha used a parable of a cart being dismantled. Even when reassembled, it is no longer the original cart. Others have likened this process to what occurs when one lit candle is used to ignite another candle: The second flame originated from the first with exactly the same qualities as that origin, yet it is a new flame.

The Buddha also rejected the Hindu notion that animal sacrifices are a necessary component of worship. In fact, he told his followers not to kill any living thing. (Many Buddhists have interpreted this teaching as a call for vegetarianism, although accounts of his life indicate that the Buddha himself ate meat.) The Buddha further argued that professional priests are unnecessary because people are capable of discovering and interpreting religious truth on their own. Both of these positions naturally alienated those Hindus who made their livings as priests, because priests were not only in charge of animal sacrifices but also responsible for providing guidance in all spiritual matters. However, the opposition of India's priests did not dampen the public's enthusiasm for the Buddha, who quickly became a popular public figure.

Providing Guidance

For about forty-five years after his Deer Park Sermon, the Buddha expanded on Buddhist theology while encouraging the spread of his ideas by walking from village to village, town to town, and city to city in central-northern India, teaching dharma to all who would listen. His listeners included people of both genders and all levels of society, regardless of caste. Throughout his travels, he emphasized that he was a human being, not a god, and never told his followers to worship him. In fact, he did not ask that people obey any god, or even acknowledge the existence of a god; however, he did not deny the existence of a god either. Instead, the Buddha urged people to follow their own paths to spirituality rather than following someone else's. He viewed himself as a guide rather than a leader;

The First Buddhist Nuns

Four years after the Buddha's enlightenment, his aunt, Mahapajapati, came to him with five hundred women, all former wives of men who had entered the Buddha's Saṅgha. She told him she and her companions wanted to enter the Saṅgha too. At the time, there was no such thing as a Buddhist nun, and the Buddha refused to listen to her request. Buddhist master Sherab Chödzin Kohn, in his book with Samuel Bercholz An Introduction to the Buddha and His Teachings, *tells the story of what happened next.*

Mahapajapati, thinking that if the women showed courage and determination, the Buddha would not be able to refuse them, decided to gather them together and follow the Buddha to Vaishali [the city where he was going to preach]. The women had their hair cut, put on saffron-colored robes, took alms bowls, and set off on foot. Many of them were pampered noblewomen with soft hands and feet. When they arrived, Mahapajapati went to the Kutagara Hall [where the Buddha would be speaking] and stood waiting outside, hoping for an opportunity to see the Blessed One. Her feet were sore and swollen, she was covered with dust, and she was nearly sobbing with exhaustion. Ānanda [the Buddha's cousin] found her and . . . was filled with pity and sympathy at the sight of her. Ānanda . . . told [the Buddha] of Mahapajapati. . . . The Buddha said, "Enough, Ānanda. Do not ask that women be allowed to enter the order."

According to Kohn, it was only after much pleading that Ānanda *convinced the Buddha to relent and allow Mahapajapati and her female companions to become the first Buddhist nuns. However, the Buddha admitted from the outset that women were just as capable of achieving enlightenment as men.*

in other words, his role was to help others continue in the right direction, not to tell people precisely where to place their footsteps on the path to enlightenment.

Nevertheless, from the outset the Buddha attracted large numbers of devoted followers. In one town, more than fifty people converted to Buddhism; in another, over two hundred. Many of these converts left their parents, spouses, or other family members behind to remain with the Buddha, much as Siddhārtha

Gautama had left his family behind to become the Buddha.

Ordination Ceremonies

Eventually, however, the Buddha returned to the palace to visit his father. There he reconciled with Shuddhodana, although Shuddhodana at first expressed some anger over his son's decision to become a holy man. Shuddhodana was also upset because the Buddha converted his half-brother Nanda and son Rahula to Buddhism without consulting him, since both young men were Shuddhodana's heirs. After the Buddha ordained Nanda and Rahula into his ministry, Shuddhodana convinced him to promise that he would never again ordain someone without parental consent. (Later, the Buddha's cousin Ānanda, his aunt Mahapajapati, his former wife Yashodhara, and even Shuddhodana himself became Buddhists as well.)

People ordained into the Buddha's ministry became monks and nuns in the Sangha, the Buddhist community. (The word *Sangha* means "crowd" or "host" and is used to refer both to all Buddhist monks and nuns and to small communities of monks and nuns.) At first, the ordination into the Sangha consisted of a person making a commitment to follow the Buddha and his teachings and the Buddha accepting that person as a follower.

Later, however, the Buddha established a formal ordination ceremony, requiring the incipient monk to shave his hair and beard, put on a yellow robe, and recite these words three times: "I go for refuge to the Buddha; I go for refuge to the *dharma*; I go for refuge to the *sangha*."[19] These three sources of refuge—the Buddha, the dharma, and the Sangha—are called the Three Jewels; taking refuge means relying on the Three Jewels for guidance and inspiration.

Along with making the ordination ceremony more complex, the Buddha commanded his disciples not only to wander throughout India teaching his dharma but also to ordain people as part of their duties. He said to them: "Go now, monks, and wander, for the gain of many people, for the welfare of many people, out of compassion for the world, for the good, the gain, and the welfare of gods and men."[20] As a result of this pronouncement, unlike the first sixty Buddhist disciples who were ordained by the Buddha himself, many subsequent disciples became Buddhists without ever meeting the Buddha. This dramatically and quickly increased the number of Buddhists, because even though the Buddha could not be in many places at once, his disciples could.

Wanderers

The first Buddhist monks were homeless wanderers who begged for their food. During the dry season, they would travel individually or in small groups and sleep in the open; during the rainy season, they would congregate in large groups and stay in one place, usually under the shelter of a grove of trees, waiting for the rains to end so they could travel again. Whether traveling or encamped, though, they continued to teach the dharma, to meditate, to beg for their food, and to offer emotional support for the many people who decided to join them.

As the number of these people grew, the monks developed rules to guide their conduct, requiring followers to recite these rules daily and confess whether they had broken any of them. Modern scholars disagree on the text of these recitations, although most agree that their purpose must have been to remind the monks of their commitment to Buddhism.

For several years after sending his monks to teach his dharma, the Buddha himself continued to wander as well. He traveled throughout northern India, but he never went more than 250 miles from Isipatana, where he had preached his first sermon. He spent most of his time in major cities, probably because it gave him access to the largest number of people. In the last twenty or twenty-five rainy seasons of his life, he remained sheltered in Śrāvastī, a large, wealthy city situated at the crossroads of two major trade routes. There, one of his disciples offered him the use of a glade where he and his followers could shelter themselves from the weather.

The Buddha's Death

At the age of eighty, the Buddha fell ill while in the urban city of Vaiśālī. It is believed that his illness was caused by eating tainted food—perhaps spoiled pork—and the resulting dysentery weakened him to the point of death. Within a short time (accounts of the duration vary), he died in a grove in the city of Kuśinagarī, and his body was cremated seven days later. According to some reports, the Buddha's last words were "All compounded things are liable to decay, strive with mindfulness."[21]

Prior to his death, the Buddha had specifically commanded that no individual was to succeed him as the head of the religion he had founded. He also wanted the religion to be decentralized, without any one force tying its many components together. To this end, the Buddha supposedly said to his cousin, "So, Ānanda, whether now or after my decease, whoever you are, you must remain as islands to

The Buddha's death (depicted on the right), his funeral ceremony (middle of the left side), and his cremation (top left) are depicted in this eighteenth-century painting.

yourselves, as defences to yourselves with the Dharma as your island and the Dharma as your defence, remaining unconcerned with other islands and other defences."[22] After the Buddha's death, his disciples intentionally left the religion leaderless.

Without strong direction, Buddhism soon split into many factions as its followers disagreed about the best way to interpret the Buddha's teachings. However, regardless of how many variations of the religion developed, the essence of the Buddha's message remained undiluted: People should become self-aware, learn mental discipline, avoid harming others, abandon destructive feelings and behaviors, develop beneficial feelings and attitudes toward the self and others, and act and think in constructive ways while questioning and testing every idea. Today, the Buddha's words continue to encourage people to better themselves and society.

chapter three

The Development of Buddhism in India

After the Buddha's death, his followers struggled to keep his religion viable without its leader. As part of this struggle, they expanded on Buddhist scripture, interpreting and reinterpreting the Buddha's teachings in accordance with their own memories of his words and their convictions about their meaning. Despite the efforts of his followers, divisions soon arose regarding the Buddha's message.

Reconstructing the Buddha's Message

Right after the Buddha's death, five hundred of his disciples gathered to honor his transcendence with a recitation of his teachings. Their meeting at the city of Rājagrha, which is known as the First Council, established a set body of the Buddha's discourses—the Dharma-Vinaya (or "Teachings-Discipline"). The First Council may have also resulted in the first detailed code of conduct—or monastic code—for Buddhist monks and nuns. However, none of this material was written down; instead, the council's goal was to establish

After the Buddha's death, his disciples struggled to interpret his teachings based on their own memories of his words.

an oral tradition and make sure that the Buddha's words were passed on accurately.

Not everyone, however, was pleased with this effort. In particular, a monk named Purāna, who had indoctrinated about five hundred disciples, refused to endorse the First Council's work, saying that he did not need anyone else to tell him what the Buddha had said. Moreover, modern scholars disagree about the true nature of the First Council. Andrew Skilton, in his *Concise History of Buddhism*, says,

The First Council is important, for it shows the early Saṅgha trying to organize itself, and establish its own identity and continuity, with a definitive body of discourses and regulations, its own Dharma and Vinaya. . . . It also suggests that Rājagṛha was a major centre for the early Saṅgha, where there was a sufficient concentration of the Buddha's disciples and sufficient support in terms of food and shelter for such a meeting to take place. However, there remains considerable doubt as to whether such a meeting as described, a rather grand and imposing affair, could have taken place within the time and distances involved. . . . Moreover, it is quite clear that parts of the collections of the discourses and monastic regulations . . . date from a much later period than this. What seems very likely is that a number of the Buddha's disciples came together, and made some attempt to pool their recollection of his various discourses, perhaps arranged according to their style and content, and recited together some form of [the Buddha's teachings]. . . . Finally, it is clear from the incident involving Purāna that there were those who chose not to participate in these regularizing activities, and did not accept them.[23]

Scholars are even more unsure about the nature of a second council, which apparently took place in about 345 B.C., roughly sixty years (although some scholars say one hundred) after the Buddha's death. The Second Council convened at the insistence of monks who believed that members of the Sangha in the city of Vaiśālī were breaking the monastic code. Specifically, one group of monks accused another of eating at inappropriate times, engaging in complex monetary transactions, and enjoying sensual pleasures. As a result of these accusations, the Second Council restated the rules that monks and nuns should observe, scolded the transgressors, and then disbanded.

The Worthy Ones

Approximately thirty-seven years later, another council—which most Buddhists call the Pātaliputra Council but some call the Third Council—convened in the city of Pātaliputra. The council addressed issues related to the arhat, or "worthy ones," who were said to have broken the ten fetters, or restraints, that hinder enlightenment: (1) a belief in separate selfhood, (2) skeptical doubt, (3) an attachment to rules and rituals for their own sake, (4) sexual desire, (5) ill will toward others, (6) a desire to remain within the world of form, (7) a desire to exist in the world of formlessness, (8) conceit, (9) restlessness, and (10) ignorance.

There were 499 arhat living on earth at the time of the Buddha's death. By the time of the Third Council, a Buddhist monk named Mahādeva was teaching that the arhat could experience temptation

One of the sixteen original arhat, who were said to have broken the ten fetters that hinder enlightenment, is depicted here.

and uncertainty, could exhibit ignorance, and may have needed help in breaking their fetters. This position angered Buddhists who believed the arhat to be beyond such flaws. Consequently, they called for a meeting to discuss Mahādeva's teachings, and during this meeting a schism arose between the pro- and anti-Mahādeva forces. (Some historians believe that this schism actually developed during the Second Council over other issues and that the two camps

The Buddhist monk Mahādeva, shown at the bottom of this stone carving, taught that arhat did not necessarily have to break all their fetters, causing a split among the faithful.

merely became more hardened in opposition because of the Mahādeva affair; others believe that the schism took place much later than the time of the Third Council.)

The two groups became the Mahāsangha and the Sthaviras sects. The Mahāsangha ("Greater Community") followed the teachings of Mahādeva, while the Sthaviras ("Elders") argued that their beliefs reflected the true teachings of the Buddha. Eventually, in addition to these two sects—also called schools, traditions, or orders—at least sixteen other sects developed in India, each with its own version of the Buddha's teachings or its own interpretation of those teachings.

Oral Tradition

One reason for this variety is Buddhism's initial reliance on oral tradition. Because the Buddha's teachings were passed on orally, there was no single text to guide Buddhists in the practice of their religion. Moreover, the religion itself promoted the idea that lessons learned through oral tradition were more significant than those learned from a book:

> A special tradition outside the scriptures;
>
> Not founded on words and letters;

Lineages

Even after the emergence of Buddhist scripture, Buddhism continued to emphasize the importance of transmitting teachings orally rather than in writing. As part of this emphasis, Buddhists have always supported the existence of lineages—lines of succession from one Buddhist teacher, or master, to another. In continuing his line of succession, a master chooses the person who will follow him, having verified that the chosen one had indeed achieved enlightenment. Consequently, a student who learns from a Buddhist master and then becomes a master himself can trace his wisdom back to the Buddha, who is considered the first master, or patriarch, of many. For example, the twenty-eighth patriarch was Bodhidharma, who carried his lineage from India to China in the sixth century A.D., where it died out after his fifth successor failed to name the next master.

Pointing directly to the heart of man;

Seeing into one's own nature and attaining Buddhahood.[24]

In fact, most Buddhists believe that oral tradition is still essential to Buddhism. As Rupert Gethin explains in his book *The Foundations of Buddhism*, "Practical training [in Buddhism] is difficult to impart and acquire simply on the basis of theoretical manuals; one needs a teacher who can demonstrate the training and also comment on and encourage one in one's own attempts to put the instructions into practice."[25] Gethin also notes that the Buddha himself spoke against relying on texts as a way to understand the religion:

The Buddha regarded the Dharma he had found as "profound, hard to see, hard to understand, peaceful, sublime, beyond the sphere of mere reasoning, subtle, to be experienced by the wise." Thus knowledge of Dharma is not something that is acquired simply by being told the necessary information or by reading the appropriate texts. Knowledge of Dharma is not a matter of scholarly and intellectual study. This does not mean that such study may not have a part to play, yet it can never be the whole story. In fact, according to an ancient and authoritative view of the matter, knowledge of Dharma comes about as a result of the interplay between three kinds of understanding (*prajñā/paññā*): that which arises from listening (*sruta/suta*), that which arises from reflection (*cintā*), and that which arises from spiritual practice (*bhāvanā*).[26]

Initially, Buddhists passed on the Buddha's words as well as stories that illustrated certain aspects of his teachings. One of the best-known Buddhist stories is the mustard seed parable, which relates to Buddhist teachings regarding the need to face and accept suffering. In this story, a woman named Kisa Gautami carries her newly deceased child to the Buddha, begging him to bring the boy back to life whether through medicine or magic. Understanding that the woman is not ready to hear the truth—and that in fact she has to discover it for herself—he sends her on a mission, saying, "Yes, I can help you. First you must bring me a mustard seed, but it must come from a house in which no death has ever taken place." For an entire day the woman searches for such a house but finds none. She then returns to the Buddha and says, "I know now that I am not alone in my grief. Death is common to all people."[27]

Buddhist scripture also includes stories about the Buddha's former lives. Called the Jātaka tales, some of them relate to lifetimes when he was an animal instead of a human. For example, the "Hare Jātaka" tells about his life as a hare, during which he was so generous that he vowed to sacrifice his own flesh if a beggar needed food. In all, the Buddha was said to have told about 550 of his previous states of existence, and there is a Jātaka tale about each one.

Written Scripture

Over time, these and other stories became part of a written Buddhist scripture, known today as the Buddhist canon. These scriptures consist of thousands of books created by various Buddhist teachers in the centuries after the Buddha's death. These books contain basic Buddhist teachings, interpretations of those teachings, and what people believe to be the historical words of the Buddha. The Buddhist canon has three parts—the Vinaya Pitaka, the Sūtra Pitaka, and the Abhidharma Pitaka—and is therefore typically referred to as Tripitaka or Tipitaka, "the three baskets."

The Vinaya Pitaka consists of writings relating to how Buddhist monks and nuns should behave. The Sūtra Pitaka consists of the Buddha's sūtras, written down after the Buddha's death by people who had memorized them. The Abhidharma

Pitaka consists of explanatory material. Some schools of Buddhism have additional pitakas or different versions of them. There are seven different Vinaya Pitakas, for example, that have survived to the present. Various schools of Buddhism consult different texts, and people are encouraged to use the texts as a guide rather than as a representation of religious authority.

There is also another collection of sutras, the Mahāyāna Sūtras, that appeared over many centuries, beginning in the first century B.C. Some Buddhists believe that both the Sūtra Pitaka and the Mahāyāna Sūtras represent the true teachings of the historical Buddha, with the Sūtra Pitaka being the Buddha's words as originally spoken to mortal human beings and the Mahāyāna Sūtras his words

A monk reads from a book in the Tripitaka, the Buddhist canon.

as originally spoken to divine and exalted beings while the Buddha was on another level of existence.

The Bodhisattvas

The Mahāyāna Sūtras introduced a new element into Buddhism: the idea that there are many bodhisattvas, or buddhas-to-be. Buddhists who practice some form of Mahāyāna Buddhism, believe that anyone can become a buddha by achieving full enlightenment and that a bodhisattva is a person who has made a serious commitment to this path, which can take many lifetimes. Mahāyāna Buddhists generally believe that each rebirth brings a bodhisattva to an ever-higher realm of existence; by the eighth rebirth, the buddha-to-be can return to the ordinary realm of existence in any form to teach mortal human beings.

At any stage of development, bodhisattvas are committed to helping others. In fact, they believe it is better for a buddha to remain among ordinary mortals, teaching them the dharma, than to dwell in nirvāna, which they believe is an emptiness rather than a place. According to Mahāyāna Buddhist scripture, the Buddha himself gave up his chance to dwell in nirvāna in order to help people.

A separate branch of the Mahayana tradition, Vajrayana—which some scholars consider to be an entirely different tradition rather than a variation of Mahayana—was started by Mahayana Buddhists who believed that a bodhisattva could attain enlightenment in just one lifetime. The Vajrayanists created texts called *sadhanas* in which they told exactly what a person would have to do in order to achieve this single-life accomplishment. Over time, Vajraya Buddhism (also known as Tantric Buddhism or Buddhist Tantrism) also included ideas about how certain expressions of human sexuality might lead to enlightenment. Some scholars believe that these ideas had their roots in the goddess and earth religions of ancient India, in which interactions between feminine and masculine powers were considered an important part of spirituality.

The Changing Sangha

Mahayana Buddhism began to develop during the Buddha's lifetime, but most variations in Buddhism occurred after his death, in large part because of the changing nature of the Saṅgha. Whereas the Buddha's original monks had been wanderers, as the religion grew it attracted wealthy patrons who donated land and buildings where Buddhist monks and nuns could settle permanently in monasteries and nunneries. At first, the members of the Saṅgha stayed at these places only during the rainy season, when travel was not possible; gradually, however, they lived there year-round. By the end of the first century after the Buddha's death few members of the Saṅgha were homeless wanderers. As a result, people no longer first heard the teachings of the Buddha from monks visiting their own villages. As time passed, the only way a person could hear the Buddha's teachings was by visiting a monastery, where monks routinely recited the dharma and taught meditation.

This change altered the nature of Buddhism in several ways. First, it encouraged the development of many geographically distinct Saṅghas. As monks translated the Buddha's words into local dialects and languages, their meaning sometimes changed slightly, and new interpretations of the Buddha's teachings developed. Historian Andrew Skilton believes that the likelihood of such errors occurring was present from the beginning of Buddhism:

This situation was in a sense encouraged by the Buddha himself, in that he refused to allow his teaching to be standardized into any particular dialect or format. Without a [single language] in which the Dharma could be transmitted, the resulting variety of languages may have contributed to mutual misunderstanding, and more certainly to differing interpretations of doctrinal issues.[28]

Sometimes, however, divergence from Buddhist doctrine was intentional. This occurred when a particular group of monks disagreed with members of their local or regional Saṅgha over how the Buddha's teachings should be interpreted and split off to form their own Buddhist community. Many Indian Buddhists considered these adversarial splits to be a crime, however, akin to killing someone, because collectively the members of the Saṅgha feared that repeated splits might eventually destroy their religion.

Another by-product of the end of monastic wandering was that it provided Buddhists with a place of worship—monastery buildings—and with this came a tendency to conduct more rituals. Many people left offerings for the Buddha or sang hymns to him at such places; others erected monuments there in his honor. In addition, many monasteries housed the Buddha's relics—things he once touched in life—which were increasingly venerated. Monasteries also became places where lay followers not only visited but lived in order to be close to the monks who taught the dharma. As a result, monastery

In the beginning, Buddhist monasteries, like the one pictured here, provided shelter for wandering monks, but gradually monks became more settled and monasteries became places of worship.

buildings increased in size, and monastic codes of conduct and ordination ceremonies became more complex.

Important Patrons

The trend toward Buddhist monks becoming settled in monasteries could have put an end to the spread of Buddhism. Most monasteries were concentrated in the region where the Buddha himself taught—known today as the Indian state of Bihar—and the religion could easily have failed to extend beyond this region. However, in 268 B.C. Buddhism gained a powerful promoter when Aśoka Maurya

assumed the throne of a mighty Indian empire originally established by his grandfather.

Eight years after becoming emperor, Aśoka Maurya sent his armies to quell a rebellion in eastern India. The bloodshed was so massive there that it preyed on Emperor Aśoka's mind. This made him receptive to the teachings of a Buddhist monk he encountered shortly after the end of the war. The monk preached nonviolence, and soon Emperor Aśoka became a Buddhist. He ordered that words promoting peace be carved on rocks throughout his kingdom. For example,

Do not perform sacrifices or do anything else that might hurt animals. . . . Be generous to your friends. . . . Do not get involved in quarrels and arguments. . . . Try to be pure of heart, humble and faithful. . . . Do not think only of your good points; remember also your faults as well and try to put them right.[29]

Aśoka Maurya not only became a Buddhist but also actively promoted the religion by founding new monasteries, visiting religious sites, meeting with Buddhist monks, and giving them gifts. At the same time, he encouraged people to practice Buddhism without necessarily becoming monks. Had he not done this, Buddhism might have become dominated by a class of professional priests. Instead, during Aśoka's reign, Buddhism became a religion for everyone, not just for those who were willing to leave their families and live in a monastery. Tales based on Buddhist principles consequently appeared in Indian folklore, and most people became familiar with Buddhist teachings.

In fact, Buddhism became such an integral part of Indian life during

Shortly after Aśoka Maurya became a Buddhist he ordered rock carvings such as these to promote his new faith.

Emperor Aśoka's reign that it remained a strong religion even after his death. By this time, the emperor had also fostered the spread of Buddhism outside of India, sending monks to preach in other lands just as the Buddha had once sent monks to preach throughout India. Aśoka Maurya's missionaries went in all directions, carrying the Buddha's teachings throughout Asia, the Middle East, and northern Africa, and the religion prospered.

The End of Buddhism in India

Yet despite Aśoka Maurya's efforts, even as Buddhism was growing in non-Indian countries, it was slowly dying in India. Part of the reason for this was the fact that the Buddha had incorporated Hindu beliefs into his religion. Indians were so comfortable with these familiar elements that they increasingly emphasized them over other aspects of Buddhism. Gradually, people began to equate the Buddha with a Hindu deity, worshiping him in much the same way. Meanwhile, as members of the Sangha cloistered themselves in monasteries and nunneries, they ceased to win over new converts.

The final blow to Buddhism in India occurred when the Muslims began to invade the country from Turkey in the eighth century. Their religion of Islam made inroads into the country, and after a series of massive invasions in the twelfth and thirteenth centuries, the Ganges River basin was under complete control of Islamic rulers. Many of these invaders mistook India's monasteries for fortresses; they therefore destroyed these buildings, killing their occupants and burning their manuscripts. During these foreign invasions, Buddhist refugees fled from India into the countries of Burma, Tibet, and elsewhere in Southeast Asia. Buddhism was well established in these places, but in Siddhārtha Gautama's home country, few continued to follow his teachings.

chapter | four

The Spread of Buddhism

Because Buddhist missionaries from India took the dharma to most parts of Asia and beyond, Buddhism did not disappear with its demise in India. However, as the religion was transplanted in new places, it took on new aspects that reflected the practices of local cultures. No longer was Buddhism a monolithic faith; now there were varieties of Buddhism peculiar to this place or that, each one offering slightly different ideas about the nature of enlightenment and the way people should act in order to attain it.

Theravada

As Buddhism spread, three traditions, Theravāda, Mahāyāna, and Vajrayāna, became dominant, depending on location. Of the three main branches of Buddhism, only Theravāda originated as part of India's original eighteen schools. However, it did not blossom until after it was transported out of India and into Sri Lanka in the third century B.C. One reason for its rapid growth in Sri Lanka was the fact that monks there decided to write Theravāda scriptures down. The first Buddhists to supplement their oral tradition with a written doctrine, these monks spent three years, from 35 to 32 B.C., completing their task.

A Pāli Chant

The Pāli canon includes chants related to the Buddha's teachings. One such chant addresses the Buddhist idea of impermanence:

All things are impermanent
They arise and they pass away.
To live in harmony with this truth
Brings great happiness.

According to Theravāda teachings, the process of creating written Buddhist scripture began with the Fourth Council which was held in Sri Lanka. At this meeting, monks recalled, discussed, recited, interpreted, and memorized the Buddha's teachings in preparation for their writings. They also agreed to use the language of Pāli—an ancient, Indian language similar to Sanskrit—for their scripture, even though the Buddha himself probably spoke Magadhi (a language named for the kingdom of Magadha, where it originated). Consequently, Theravāda scripture is known as the Pāli canon.

The Pāli canon is the only Buddhist scripture to survive in its original language. However, the current version, made up of roughly fifty medium-sized volumes, was created in Sri Lanka in the fifth century A.D. and differs from the first version. Specifically,

it includes commentaries by six, fifth-century Buddhist teachers and might also contain alterations of the Buddha's words as recited by those attending the Fourth Council.

Perhaps because it was the first Buddhist tradition to be committed to writing, Theravāda Buddhism relies on a fairly literal interpretation of the historic Buddha's words, and many scholars believe it to be the most accurate representation of the Buddha's original teachings and practices. It emphasizes meditation and the development of wisdom and self-awareness in accordance with a collection of the Buddha's teachings known as the Abhidharma. Rupert Gethin, in his book *The Foundations of Buddhism*, summarizes the Theravādan view of how these teachings came about:

It is told by some that after the Buddha gained awakening he sat beneath the tree of awakening for seven days contemplating the Dharma which he had penetrated. Then he got up from his seat and for seven days he stood gazing with unblinking eyes at the seat thinking, "On this seat I gained knowledge." At that time the gods thought that perhaps the Buddha still had something to accomplish as it appeared he had not abandoned attachment to the seat of awakening. So the Buddha performed the miracle of the pairs, emitting streams of fire and water from every pore of his body. Then for seven days he walked up and down between the seat of awakening and where he had been standing. Now, twenty-one days after he had gained awakening, he sat in the House of Jewels, so called because here, over seven days, he conceived the seven books of the Abhidharma—the jewels of the Dharma. On the seventh day, when he began to contemplate the contents of the seventh book, the Great Book, his body began to emit rays of six colours: blue, yellow, red, white, maroon, clear. And as he contemplated this infinite and immeasurable Dharma, the rays emitted from his body lit up the earth, the waters, and the skies. They lit up the realms of the gods and flooded beyond throughout billions of world systems.[30]

For Buddhists in Theravāda traditions, Abhidharma refers not only to the Buddha's words—whether oral or written—but also to the system of thought that those words represent. According to Gethin, "Hearing it being recited—even without understanding it—can have a far-reaching effect. The Abhidharma catches the very essence of the Dharma, which means that its sound can operate almost as a charm or spell."[31]

Government Support for Theravada

The first writings of Theravada Buddhism were inspired by the teachings of the Buddhist monk Mahinda, the son of Emperor Aśoka of India. Mahinda brought Buddhism to Sri Lanka and converted its king, Devānaṁpiyatissa (called King Tissa by some historians), in 240 B.C. Under King Devānaṁpiyatissa, Buddhism became the national religion, and many monasteries were built throughout the country. This level of government support not only continued for centuries in Sri Lanka but also became the norm throughout Southeast Asia.

In Myanmar, for example, Indian missionaries introduced various types of Buddhism beginning in the first century. However, Theravāda Buddhism quickly became the most popular, in part because in the eleventh century, Myanmar's King Anawrata became an active proponent of Theravāda Buddhism, having been converted to the religion by a Theravāda Buddhist monk named Shin Arahan. The king promoted Theravāda Buddhism among his subjects, building numerous temples and pagodas (towers of several stories, usually with upward-sloping eaves) dedicated to Buddhist worship.

Similarly, in the thirteenth century, Thailand's King Rama Khamheng converted to Theravāda Buddhism and made it his country's official religion. So great was the impact of Buddhism in Thailand that in the

A Buddhist shrine marks where the Buddhist monk Mahinda met with King Devānaṁpiyatissa and introduced Buddhism to Sri Lanka.

The Stupa of Java

The nation of Indonesia, made up of several islands, does not support Buddhism at all, but there are still a few Buddhists living there. However, at one time, Indonesia was as strongly Buddhist as other Southeast Asian countries, and it contains the largest Buddhist monument in the world, a stupa on the island of Java. A stupa is a structure shaped like a mound or dome, typically built to house relics or statues of the Buddha. The earliest versions, which appeared in India and were constructed of mud, were fairly small and simple. Over time, stupas became large and elaborate, similar to temples, and they employed brick or stone.

The stupa on Java was built in the Borobodur, or "Monastery of Accumulated Virtue," and has six square terraces topped by three circular terraces with a small dome at the pinnacle. Near the bottom of the exterior walls of the lower terraces, there are carvings of people being born and reborn. Above these are carvings depicting the life of Siddhārtha Gautama prior to his enlightenment, as well as carvings of well-known bodhisattvas, or buddhas-to-be, in the Mahāyāna tradition. Images of the Buddha are carved on the circular terraces. The dome at the top of the stupa, which is similar to a small mud stupa used to house the Buddha's ashes, has no carvings, to represent the emptiness of nirvāṇa. The Borobodur stupa is therefore symbolic of the progression that a Mahayānā Buddhist makes to reach enlightenment. In all, there are seventy stupas at Borobodur, most of them decorated with carvings and housing statues of the Buddha. All of them draw hundreds of Buddhist pilgrims each year.

fourteenth century, King Lu Thai was ordained as a Theravāda Buddhist monk. Despite Theravāda's official status, from the writings of this period, historians know that Theravāda coexisted with other forms of Buddhism, some of which subsequently gained support by members of the royal family. Nonetheless, Theravāda remained popular with the public.

This same split between Buddhism, as it was practiced by kings and by the populace, occurred in Cambodia, where Buddhism gained royal backing as early as the fifth century A.D. As was the case in Thailand, the people favored Theravāda, which had been introduced by missionaries from Thailand. Unlike Thailand, however, Cambodia's kings favored Mahāyāna Buddhism.

Mahayānā Buddhism

As with Theravāda, Mahāyāna Buddhism began in India but did not

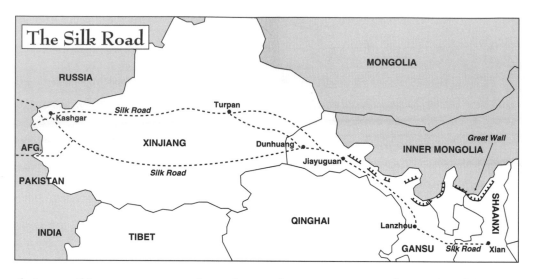

The Silk Road

thrive until it was transported to other countries, where it began to incorporate many new and complex ideas. To a greater extent than Theravada, Mahāyāna tended to interpret the Buddha's teachings loosely, and as it spread, a number of alternate versions of the Mahāyāna tradition developed. What all types of Mahāyāna Buddhism have in common, though, is that they stress the importance of compassion, believing that cultivating a concern for others is the way to attain freedom from ego. As one Mahayana text says, "And he who hopes for the welfare of the world thinks to himself: Let me undertake religious practice, that I may bring welfare and happiness to all beings."[32]

Chinese Buddhism

Most of the influence on the development of Mahāyāna Buddhism,

however, came from the Chinese, who gradually created their own versions of the religion. The Buddha's teachings reached this country sometime in the first century A.D., probably with missionaries and merchants traveling a land route known as the Silk Trade Route.

The first Buddhist monks to come to China were Mahāyāna Buddhists from Central Asia. A ruler in that region, King Kaniska (who also ruled Kashmir, northwest India, northern Pakistan, Afghanistan, and eastern Iran), sent such missionaries throughout Asia, and he established centers of Buddhist learning as oases all along the Silk Trade Route. He also built many large monasteries, encouraged new writings about the Buddha's life and teachings, and ordered the creation of the first artwork to represent the Buddha.

When King Kaniska's missionaries first arrived in China, however, they had little effect on the Chinese people as a whole. In part this was because the Central Asian monks spent their time translating Buddhist texts into Chinese rather than actively preaching to the people. These translations took many years, during which many changes and additions were made. In fact, the Chinese Tripitaka (*San-tsang*), or "Great Treasury of Sūtras" (*Ta-tsang-ching*) as it is also known, evolved over a period of more than a thousand years. It includes not only all Chinese translations of Buddhist sūtras, completed over several centuries, but also many Chinese essays on Buddhist ideas. The first printed version of the Chinese Tripitaka was completed in 983. Employing more than 130,000 wooden blocks in the printing process, it contained more than a thousand works. However, sixth-century descriptions of the Chinese Tripitaka told of approximately two thousand works. During the eighth century, when Chinese Buddhist monks invented more sophisticated printing methods, more written works were added to the Chinese Tripitaka.

Ironically, Buddhism's growth in China was aided by invasions by the Huns in approximately 320 A.D. These invaders, hoping to ease their conquest by breaking the Chinese people's ties to the past, encouraged the growth of Buddhism at the expense of traditional Confucian beliefs. Hun rulers therefore built monasteries and encouraged Buddhist monks to come into China.

Meanwhile in the south, many upper-class, educated Chinese became interested in the new religion. Soon, many of them had adopted Buddhism, although they typically integrated Chinese ideas, such as the belief in an indestructible soul and in nirvana as a form of immortality. Eventually, these new types of Buddhism were adopted by people in the lower classes as well.

By about A.D. 400, there were approximately two thousand monasteries in south China. In the early sixth century, the Chinese emperor Wu (502–549) became a Buddhist and offered royal support of the religion. During Wu's reign, a Buddhist school called Ch'an was established by the Indian monk Bodhidharma; this school, which emphasizes personal effort and centers around the practice of meditation, soon became one of the most popular forms of Buddhism in the region.

Chinese Missionaries

Eventually, during the late sixth century, Buddhism became China's primary religion. As such, it was promoted by most emperors. Some rulers built state temples, where Buddhist rituals were performed on behalf of the entire country. Similarly, Buddhist monasteries became places where people could go to receive a variety of benefits, including medical care and free food for the poor. The monastery system thrived, and the Chinese Saṅgha grew powerful. A census taken in China in the year 729 indicates that there were 126,000 monks and nuns in the country.

Around this time, Chinese schools of Buddhism fell into two categories: those that relied almost exclusively on Indian Buddhist teachings (although many disagreements arose over which of the many Buddhist texts that China imported most truly reflected the Buddha's sūtras) and those that

In late sixth century China, Buddhist monasteries became places where people could go to receive benefits such as medical care and food for the poor.

included many uniquely Chinese ideas. Interestingly, it was not unusual for a Chinese Buddhist to change schools, and, even within schools, worship practices might vary widely among the faithful.

For example, within the Ch'an, a uniquely Chinese school, Buddhists disagreed on whether a person's enlightenment, or awakening, would come on suddenly or gradually. Some argued that a person achieving enlightenment would experience a growing awareness, while others countered that ultimate truth is something a person sees all at once rather than in parts. Eventually, those who argued in favor of sudden awakening predominated. However, because of this and other ideological splits, by the ninth century there were at least five different schools of Ch'an Buddhism in China.

Chinese missionaries carried these and other types of Buddhism to other countries, aided by the same trade routes that had once brought Buddhism into China. Via the Silk Trade Route, for example, the Chinese carried their own versions of Buddhism to Pakistan, Afghanistan, Iran, Central Asia, Kashmir, and Persia. Some of these countries were not particularly eager to adopt Chinese Buddhism. Persia appears to have been the most resistant; in fact, modern scholars disagree as to whether any form of Buddhism was ever present there at all.

Vietnam and Korea, however, did accept Buddhism from Chinese missionaries. Vietnam encountered its first such Buddhists in approximately 189 A.D., and a steady stream of Chinese missionaries continued to arrive for many centuries. The reason for this lies in Vietnam's position on a major sea route from China to India and other parts of Southeast Asia. The many Buddhists who passed through Vietnam carried with them three types of Chinese Buddhism—Ch'an, A-Ham, and Pure Land—as well as Mahayana Buddhism, which would eventually become the country's dominant faith. Korea was also exposed to several types of Chinese Buddhism beginning in the late fourth century A.D. However, its people were particularly drawn to the Ch'an school.

Chinese and Indian missionaries also carried Mahāyāna Buddhism to Tibet. In particular, they introduced the Tibetans to Vajrayāna, or Tantric Buddhism, which had originated as a variation of Mahāyāna. Like Mahāyāna, Tantric Buddhism presents complex ideas about human existence and has a fairly loose approach to the Buddha's doctrine. However, it also includes elaborate

Tibetan monks perform the Black Hat Dance, one of the many elaborate rituals of Tantric Buddhism.

rituals, visualizations, and liturgy, emphasizing mental focus on a deity.

The End of Chinese Buddhism

As Mahāyāna Buddhism was flourishing elsewhere, however, China's enthusiasm for Buddhism was waning. The religion's decline began late in the T'ang dynasty (618–927) when Emperor Wu-tsung attacked Buddhism for being a foreign belief system. Other people also criticized Buddhism because it encouraged young men to leave their families to become monks. In Chinese culture, it was very important for a young man to marry and provide his family with male heirs. So as the number of monks increased, the monastic life was increasingly viewed

as a serious threat to the social order. Consequently, in 845 Emperor Wu-tsung ordered that all monasteries be closed and all monks and nuns return to their families to fulfill their obligations as sons, daughters, husbands, and wives.

As a result of this edict, Buddhism was soon replaced with Confucianism and Taoism as the official belief systems of China. (Emperor Wu-tsung was himself a Taoist.) Only two forms of Chinese Buddhism survived this transition, Ch'an and Pure Land. These two schools would continue to exist in China into modern times, although relatively few Chinese would declare themselves Buddhist. Elsewhere in Asia, Buddhism continued to thrive and develop, however.

chapter | five

Two Unique Paths: Tibetan and Japanese Buddhism

In modern times, Tibetan and Japanese monks have had the most influence on the spread of Buddhism. However, Tibetan and Japanese Buddhism today are different from the versions first introduced to the two countries by early Buddhist missionaries.

The Origins of Tibetan Buddhism

Buddhism first came to Tibet in the seventh century. At that time, the Tibetan king, Srong-brtsan-sgam-po, also known as Songsten Gampo (ca. 609–649), had two Buddhist wives, one from Nepal and one from China. At the time of their marriage to the king, each brought with her her own set of missionaries. The beliefs these two women brought were quite different. Nepalese Buddhism, thanks to Nepal's proximity to India, was essentially Indian Buddhism, whereas Chinese Buddhism by this time had developed its own set of beliefs. Because of this, the two groups of missionaries brought by the new Tibetan queens were continually at odds with one another over which of their interpretations of Buddhism was correct.

At his wives' urging, King Srong-brtsan-sgam-po built Buddhist temples where the two women and their missionaries could worship their respective traditions of Buddhism. Despite his backing for the imported faith, the king's subjects had no great inclination to adopt Buddhism. Tibetans had long practiced a religion of magic, shamans, evil spirits, and powerful gods, and they saw no reason to give it up; for the time being, Buddhism remained a faith for Tibet's royalty.

By the eighth century, many members of the royal court were Buddhist, but the Tibetan people as a whole still were not. King Khri-Srong-Ide-brtsan, also known as Trisong Detsen (704-797), invited Buddhist teachers from India to come to Tibet and establish a monastery. One of these teachers was Padmasambhava, a Tantric Buddhist who later became known as Guru Rimpoche. In 779 he created the first Buddhist monastery in Tibet. According to Tibetan legends, this monk succeeded because he literally fought and overcame a legion of demons who were trying to keep Buddhism from becoming established in Tibet.

Meanwhile, the Indian and Chinese forms of Buddhism introduced into Tibet by King Srong-brtsan-sgam-po's wives continued to thrive, but the two factions still could not get along. The king decided to hold a series of debates to determine which form of Buddhism would prevail. In the end, he decreed that Indian Buddhism was superior, and all practitioners of Chinese Buddhism either left Tibet or converted to Indian Buddhism.

As with other countries where the religion was introduced, over time Tibet developed many schools of Buddhism. All adhered to principles of Indian Buddhism, and gradually

Padmasambhava (center) created the first Buddhist monastery in Tibet.

A Tibetan lama interprets a Tantric inscription vital to achieving a transformation into the body and mind of a buddha.

the tradition known as Tantric Buddhism came to dominate. Within a short time, however, Tibet had developed its own unique form of Tantric Buddhism, with more of an emphasis on magic, mysticism, and human sexuality.

Tibetan Tantrism

Tibetan Tantrism has at its heart a series of guidebooks known as the Tantra, developed in India but expanded on in Tibet, which contain techniques intended to transform a person's body and mind into those of a buddha so that the person can attain enlightenment. These techniques include magic spells, occult diagrams called mandalas, special hand ges-

tures, and other mystical elements. Many of the instructions in the Tantra are so complex that only a specialist in the Tantra, known as a guru in India or a lama in Tibet, can interpret them. Lamas are therefore vital in helping a person achieve a buddha transformation. (Some other types of Buddhism also incorporate the idea that enlightenment can be achieved only through a Buddhist master's help, but none involves the level of complexity of Tantric Buddhism.)

The Tantric texts are not accessible to just anyone. John Snelling reports that this is because the occult techniques used in attempting to attain enlightenment can harm those unprepared for them. He explains:

The Tantric path has its dangers: this is repeatedly stressed in the traditional texts. Improper dabbling may cause psychic damage, perhaps blighting not merely this, but many future lives. Therefore, to prevent fools from rushing in, all manner of safety precautions have been set up. . . . [For example,] Tantric texts are written in an enigmatic "opaque" or "twilight" language that renders their contents meaningless to the uninitiated; also those initiated into Tantric cults have to uphold grave vows (*samaya*). Such measures are not merely designed to protect the unwary from getting burnt; they also protect the teachings themselves, for malpractice weakens their effectiveness: the spiritual equivalent of debasing the coinage. [33]

The Tantra also emphasizes the importance of sexuality in achieving enlightenment. According to the Tantra, there are many gods and goddesses, and the union of their masculine and feminine forces is necessary to sustain the universe. Moreover, the union of a god and a human consort, or a bodhisattva or buddha and a woman, can bring enlightenment. The tradition therefore encourages the expression of human sexuality and involves a great deal of sexual symbolism.

Tibetan doctrine also suggests that Tantric Buddhism is the highest form of Buddhism, but Buddhists must first practice Theravada Buddhism and then Mahayana Buddhism. Tibetan lamas spend fourteen to twenty years studying these first two traditions of Buddhism before turning to the Tantra, with the help of a qualified Tantric master.

The Dalai Lama

In interpreting and practicing Tantric teachings, Tibetan Buddhists have typically looked to the spiritual leader of Tibet, known as the Dalai Lama, or "Ocean of Wisdom," for guidance. Tibetan doctrine says that the first Dalai Lama was Tsong-kha-pa, who established the Dge-lugs-pa school of Tibetan Buddhism in the fifteenth century, and that every Dalai Lama since then has been a reincarnation of that person. Each time a Dalai Lama dies, Tibetans search for a child that they believe is that reincarnation, looking for boys who have been born within two years of their spiritual leader's death. Once they find him, they send the child to be educated by lamas in the ways of Tibetan Buddhism.

In 1642, a Mongol chief who had conquered Tibet converted to

Buddhism and made the Dalai Lama the ruler of the country. This meant that the Dalai Lama was not only the spiritual leader of Tibet but also its political leader as well. This remained true until 1959, when the People's Republic of China took over Tibet and forced the current Dalai Lama (born in 1935)—the fourteenth individual to hold the title—to flee to India, along with many of his followers. The Chinese army proceeded to destroy most of Tibet's twenty thousand Buddhist monasteries and temples, as well as many relics, statues, and other religious objects, and

attacked any Tibetan lamas remaining in Tibet.

Even after being forced into exile, the Dalai Lama remained a prominent religious and political leader. In the 1980s, he gave speeches in many international forums pleading the cause of Tibetans suffering under Chinese occupation, and he continues to be the object of adoration on the part of Tibet's faithful.

The Origins of Japanese Buddhism

About the same time Buddhism was being established in Tibet, it was also

The Dalai Lama flees Tibet in an ox-driven carriage following the invasion of his country by the People's Republic of China.

being established in Japan. When the Japanese first learned of Buddhism from Korean missionaries in the sixth century, they were reluctant to embrace the religion, fearing that their native gods—nature spirits called the *kami*—would be angry at them for adopting Buddhist ways. Their hesitation increased after a plague broke out in a region where a Buddhist temple had recently been built. Nonetheless, the rulers of Japan encouraged Buddhism because they hoped that if they adopted Buddhism it would bring them advances in art, literature, and the sciences, as had occurred in China.

Japan's transformation took place during the rule of Prince Shotoku Taishi (574–622). A Buddhist himself, the prince oversaw the construction of a cluster of temples that together became one of Japan's greatest Buddhist shrines, the Horuji. He also wrote extensively on Mahāyāna Buddhist doctrines.

Prince Shotoku's successor, Emperor Shomu, also supported Buddhism, building many new Buddhist monasteries in his capital city of Nara. By this time, Buddhism had become fully entrenched in Japan. There were state temples in every Japanese province, and many Buddhist monks had become powerful and wealthy members of society, involved in politics and the intrigues of the royal court.

Many of them were corrupt as well, taking money that should have gone to monasteries or temples and failing to follow Buddhist precepts.

Over the course of several hundred years, several other forms of Buddhism developed in Japan. According to scholar Andrew Skilton, all of these new schools, even those that developed from types of Buddhism imported from China, had a unique Japanese character. In particular, these new schools did not require the involvement of monks because people were tired of their corruption; instead, the new schools had simple teachings that even the uneducated could understand. Skilton summarizes the common elements of these schools:

> All the new schools shared certain features: a strong emphasis upon faith on the part of the practitioner; strong, charismatic founders dissatisfied with the established forms of Buddhism; an emphasis upon a single, practical teaching which would ensure Awakening [enlightenment]; and a popular appeal, which shifted the centre of gravity of Japanese Buddhism from the sphere of aristocratic patronage towards the populace.[34]

Pure Land Buddhism

The first new schools of Buddhism to be established in Japan in the twelfth

This sculpture of Amitabha, whose teachings established Japan's Pure Land Buddhism, depicts the monk seated in the lotus position.

century were all based on a school known as Pure Land Buddhism. This form of Buddhism, which was brought to Japan by the Chinese monk Honen (1133–1212), centers around a buddha named Amitabha (Amida in Japan) who once vowed that if he attained enlightenment he would help whoever called on him. This buddha is now said to live in the Pure Land, a paradise with many lotus blossoms (the Buddhist symbol of wisdom). Pure Land Buddhists in China believed that anyone who fol-

lowed Amitabha's teachings would eventually come to live in the Pure Land as well. In the meantime, they could call on Amitabha for help. In Japan, however, the main focus of the religion became the act of calling on the buddha rather than following his teachings. In other words, instead of believing that they had to learn and follow Amida's teachings in order to reach paradise, the Japanese believed that all they needed to do was call on Amida to help guide them there. If they did this repeatedly throughout their lives, their attainment of the Pure Land was assured. To this end, they often said "Namu Amida Butsu," or "Hail to Lord Buddha Amida."

Eventually, one of Honen's Japanese disciples, Shinran, declared that it was only necessary to say this phrase once in a single lifetime to assure a place in the Pure Land after death. Shinran believed that a person reached the Pure Land solely because of Amida's compassion, rather than because of how that person might have behaved while on earth. Therefore, Shinran thought it was unnecessary to take any Buddhist vows, live in a monastery, or even engage in established spiritual practices. As a result of his beliefs, Shinran abandoned the monastic life and married. His disciples increasingly advocated the abandonment of other Pure Land practices as well, which included vegetarianism. (This made the religion more appealing in a country where fish was a major source of food.)

Shinran's religion soon became known as the True Pure Land school, or Jōdo-shin-shū, and it influenced attitudes in other Japanese schools. Under this influence, for example, many schools deemphasized the difference between monastic and lay life and allowed their monks to marry, as Shinran had done. Similarly, some schools exposed to Shinran's teachings adopted the True Pure Land school's doctrine that it is impossible for an ordinary person to develop the meditation skills and other behaviors necessary to attain enlightenment in a single lifetime. What is needed, therefore, is the grace of Amida. This reliance on "the power of the other" (*tariki*) came to overshadow a belief in "one's own power" (*jiriki*) in many versions of Japanese Buddhism.

Zen Buddhism

In fact, meditation was one way Shinran's school of Buddhism differed from another Chinese form of Buddhism that traveled from China to Japan. Zen Buddhism, also called

A carved statue of Bodhidarma, the Indian monk who created the Ch'an school of Buddhism, which became known as Zen.

the Meditation school, was first created in China as the Ch'an school by an Indian monk, Bodhidharma, in A.D. 520. After first becoming established in Korea, several variations of Ch'an Buddhism reached Japan beginning in the seventh century, but Zen did not become a dominant Buddhist movement there for another five hundred years.

From the outset, Ch'an Buddhism required meditation, because Bodhidharma taught that meditation was the only way to know truth and therefore the only means to enlightenment. Once in Japan, however, the tradition became even more oriented toward mental exercises as opposed to the study of dharma. In fact, meditating took on so much importance that some Zen Buddhists abandon the study of the Buddha's teachings so that they can spend more time meditating. In addition, whereas in other forms of Buddhism monks do not perform physical labor, many Zen Buddhist monks welcome such labor as a way to prepare the body for meditation.

Other changes occurred as Zen Buddhism became more uniquely Japanese. When Zen Buddhism first developed in Japan, it had several variations, but over time that number was reduced to only two: Rinzai and Soto. Between the twelfth and fourteenth centuries, Rinzai became popular with the warrior, or samurai, class that then ruled Japan. Japanese peasants, on the other hand, were attracted to Soto. For hundreds of years thereafter, the Rinzai and Soto schools of Zen Buddhism developed separately in Japan, and practitioners of each form criticized the other.

Sudden vs. Gradual Enlightenment

The main point of contention between the Rinzai and Soto schools is their view on how enlightenment is achieved. Zen Buddhists of the Rinzai school believe that enlightenment comes on suddenly, whereas those of the Soto school believe that it comes on gradually. This divergence of opinion has led to a difference in how each school practices Zen Buddhism.

In particular, because the Rinzai school teaches that enlightenment can be attained in an instant, its masters try to jolt their pupils into experiencing a sudden shift in thinking that might bring about enlightenment. They do this through the koan (called *kung-an* in China), which is a problem or question, usually paradoxical, that is designed to challenge the mind and force it to consider reality in new ways. One example of a koan is "What is the sound of one hand clapping?" Another is "What was your Original Face before your parents were born?" According to the Japanese Zen Buddhist Hakuin (1686–1769), the basic purpose of koans, which seemingly have no answer, is to perplex the mind so much that it lets go of the ego, thereby readying a person for sudden enlightenment. He explains:

> If you take up one koan and investigate it without ceasing, your thoughts will die and your ego-demands will be destroyed. It is as though a vast abyss opened

Classifications of Koans

The Zen Buddhist master Hakuin (1686–1769) standardized and classified many Rinzai Zen koans, grouping them into five levels of difficulty. David Fontana, in his book Discover Zen, *offers a summary of these levels, beginning with the easiest.*

1. Hosshin koans, which give insight into emptiness, the essential essence of all things. . . . A good example is: "With hands of emptiness I take hold of the plough; while walking I ride the buffalo."

2. Kikan koans, which lead to a better understanding of the . . . world as seen through the eye of enlightenment. An example is the question "What is the meaning of Bodhidharma coming from the West?" followed by the answer "The cypress tree in the garden."

3. Gonsen koans, which help clarify the difficult words of Zen masters and open up a hidden world of beauty and wisdom. One such koan is the question "Speech and silence are concerned with subject and object. How can I transcend both subject and object?" followed by the answer "I always think of Konan [a province in China] in March. Partridges chirp among the fragrant blossoms."

4. Nanto koans, which point to a subtle place beyond all opposites and lead to tranquility amid life's vicissitudes. For example, "It is like a water buffalo passing through a window; its head, horns and four legs all pass through, why can't its tail pass?"

5. Goi koans, the most difficult of all, which are associated with verses composed by Master Tozan Ryokay, and lead to final insight into the apparent and the real. A typical example is: "In such a wide world, why put on ceremonial robes and answer the bell?"

up in front of you, with no place to put your hands and feet. You face death, and your heart feels as though it were fire. Then suddenly you are one with the koan, and body and mind let go. . . . This is known as seeing into one's own nature. You must push forward relentlessly, and with the help of this great concentration you will penetrate without fail to the infinite source of your own nature.[35]

Although the concept of the koan originated with Chinese Buddhists, the Japanese greatly added to their number and complexity. In fact, most koans used by Zen Buddhist masters today were developed after Rinzai arrived in Japan. Over time, Rinzai masters created many new koans, and when their students became masters themselves, they presented these same koans to their students. In this way, certain koans became standard. Eventually they were organized into collections, which include the Mumokan, the Hekiganroku, the Tetteki Tosui, and the Shoyoroku.

Meanwhile, the Soto school developed a variety of practices designed to gradually lead a person to enlightenment. In particular, Soto Zen Buddhists stress the importance of practicing disciplined meditation several times a day, using specific techniques and holding the body in a certain way, as a means of slowly developing physical and mental awareness. Always done while sitting, the act of meditating is known as *zazen*; *za* means "sitting" and *zen* means "meditation."

One of the most popular methods of *zazen* for practitioners of Soto Zen is wall-gazing: A person meditates while staring at a blank wall through half-closed eyelids. The idea for this practice came from a story about Bodhidharma, the founder of Ch'an Buddhism. Psychologist David Fontana relates this story in his book *Discover Zen*:

> We are told that Bodhidharma retired to a cave and meditated facing a wall for nine years. To overcome tiredness he cut off his eyelids, and the first tea plants sprang from his drops of blood. Zen does not waste time arguing over the truth or otherwise of this story. Instead, it leaves the tale to serve not only as a perfect example of dedication to practice, but also of a method of practice itself (wall-gazing), and of the good things (the tea plants) that can arise out of suffering.[36]

Soto Zen Buddhists believe that *zazen* requires great dedication and determination. Therefore, they encourage the monastic life. In fact, the founder of the school, Dogen, created the first list of monastery rules in Japan, laying out sixty-two rules in all. One of these rules is that a junior monk is not allowed to touch a senior monk; a junior monk also cannot touch his own head or body in a senior monk's presence. The idea of monastery rules, however, runs counter to the teachings of Chinese Zen Buddhism. Ch'an was not a monastic tradition, nor was Zen Buddhism at first. Instead, people studying Buddhism worked individually with Ch'an or Zen masters, incorporating Buddhism into their daily lives. It was only after some of these masters attracted large followings that certain schools of Zen Buddhism saw the benefit of a monastic community. Soto Zen was the first to promote monastic life, but Rinzai soon followed.

Nichiren

At one time, Zen Buddhism was the most popular Buddhist tradition in Japan. Today, that distinction probably belongs to Nichiren Buddhism, which developed around the same time as Rinzai and Soto Zen Buddhism. Whereas Rinzai was the preference of Japan's rulers and Soto of its peasants, Nichiren was the choice of the country's merchant class.

However, Nichiren is not a version of Zen; in fact, it was not even a transplant from China. Instead, it was the creation of a Japanese monk named Nichiren (1222–1282). Nichiren lived during a time of many natural and political disasters, and he believed that they were caused by the fact that the Japanese were not practicing Buddhism in the way the Buddha had intended it to be practiced. After

The Lotus Sutra *carved on this stone forms the basis of Nichiren Buddhism.*

examining various sutras, he decided that one particular interpretation of the Buddha's teachings, the *Lotus Sutra* or *Saddharma-Pundarika Sutra*, developed sometime between 100 B.C. and 100 A.D., was the correct one. Nichiren promoted its complex ideas and gained followers, but he was eventually exiled to the small Japanese island of Sado by Japan's rulers, who did not appreciate hearing that their own Buddhist practices were wrong.

After Nichiren's death, many Japanese became interested in his ideas. In particular, they were drawn to his claim that complex, repeated chanting would transform not only the individual but society as well. Over the ensuing centuries, Nichiren Buddhism developed into several sects, and today one of these—Nichiren Shōshū, also known as Sōka Gakkai or "Value Creating Organization"—claims to be the largest Buddhist sect in Japan, with 300,000 members. (Some scholars, however, believe that this number is actually 45,000 and that Zen's adherents still outnumber Nichiren's.) At the very least, it appears to be the fastest growing form of Buddhism in the country.

Sōka Gakkai was founded around 1930 by Tsunesaburo Makiguchi, a pacifist who was arrested for his political activism and died in prison in 1944. The Sōka sect, however, continued to thrive and in the latter half of the twentieth century became influential in Europe and America. In the United States, a Sōka organization, Soka Gakkai International, even established the Soka University of America, a California university with 125 students from 17 states and 19 foreign countries. Soka University officials expect this number to grow significantly within the next few years. This is not an unrealistic expectation, given that there has recently been a dramatic rise in Americans' interest in Japanese and Tibetan Buddhism. More Westerners are adopting Buddhism each day, despite the difficulty of integrating ancient Asian beliefs and practices with modern society.

chapter | six

Buddhist Practices

Buddhist practices vary according to the individual tradition, but certain generalities can be made about how people express Buddhist beliefs in their daily lives. After all, their religious observances and festivals stem from the same basic teachings.

Ordination

Practicing Buddhists might be monks or nuns, or they might be lay practitioners—people who follow the teachings of the Buddha without living a monastic life. Either way, though, they typically take vows upon entering the faith. These vows involve agreeing to abandon certain activities that the Buddha was known to have abandoned during his own path to enlightenment. As Tibetan Buddhist nun Thubten Chodron notes, the concept of taking these vows was "founded upon a person's commitment to steer her or his physical, verbal, and mental energies in productive directions instead of indiscriminately acting out any thought that comes to mind."[37]

There are five specific vows for lay practitioners, known as the five lay precepts. They are to abandon killing (which some, but not all, Buddhists interpret as a requirement to become a vegetarian), stealing, lying, using intoxicating substances (i.e., drugs and alcohol), and engaging in destructive sexual behavior. Agreeing to adhere to the vows to give up these things is known as taking the precepts for life. In some traditions, lay practitioners take eight precepts for life instead of five, with the additional vows being to not eat after the midday meal; to refrain from sitting on any high surface (such as a chair or bed) or expensive material; and to shun various forms of frivolity such as singing, dancing, playing music, and wearing makeup, jewelry, and perfume. Traditions that promote the idea that there are eight precepts generally believe that it is not enough to abandon destructive sexual behavior; instead, they advocate giving up all sexual behavior. In many of these traditions, how-

ever, the lay practitioner is not expected to take the eight precepts for life but for only one day, much as in some other religions the faithful might fast for a single day. In most cases, Buddhism's eight precepts are taken on days with a full or new moon and on days of Buddhist festivals.

Monks and nuns also take certain vows when they are ordained, first as a novice and then as a full member of the Saṅgha. A novice is someone who has decided to become a monk or nun—or, in the case of children, whose parents have chosen that life for them—but has not yet learned enough about Buddhism to be able to make the commitment to full

Escaping Life

Some people think that Buddhists retreat to monasteries in order to escape the harsh realities of life. However, this is not the case, as Thubten Chodron explains in her book Buddhism for Beginners.

Those who ask [whether a monastic life is a form of escapism] think that having a job, a mortgage, and a family are difficult tasks . . . but it is a much harsher reality to be honest with ourselves and to recognize our own mistaken conceptions and harmful behavior. People who meditate and pray may not be able to show a skyscraper or a paycheck as the sign of their success, but they are by no means lazy and irresponsible. Eliminating our anger, attachment, and closed-mindedness and changing our destructive physical, verbal, and emotional habits is hard work. Much effort over a long time is necessary to become a Buddha.

ordination. Children are usually brought to a monastery to become novices at the age of eight; in most traditions, however, full ordination cannot take place until the age of twenty.

Novice monks come to their ordinations with shaved heads and wearing a robe (usually saffron colored), having cast off all trappings of their life outside the monastery upon entering its doors for the first time.

Novice nuns usually wear a blouse, skirt, and belt, and if they have entered the nunnery after puberty or after having been married, they must wait two years before being fully ordained, regardless of their age.

The full ordination ceremony is typically performed by at least ten monks and requires the person being ordained to take anywhere from two hundred to three hundred precepts for life. During this ceremony, the

At least ten monks usually perform a full Buddhist ordination ceremony, like this one, in which a novice becomes a monk.

novice requests ordination three times, and after each time the assembly is given the opportunity to reject his or her ordination. Upon final acceptance, the novice is given a new name, an outer and inner robe, and a cloak.

Life in the Monastery

The life of someone who has been ordained as a monk or nun is by definition simple and routine. Monks and nuns begin their day very early with meditation. They do not eat breakfast. Instead, they go outside the monastery or nunnery to beg for offerings, chanting hymns or ringing bells while doing so. Around midday, they typically return to their monastery or nunnery to wash their feet and hands and eat. In most traditions, this will be the only meal of the day, and it is usually taken in a large room called the Sangha Hall. Afternoons are spent teaching and learning the dharma, doing chores such as cleaning and gardening, and meditating. Near the end of the day, some monasteries might invite lay practitioners into a room known as the Dharma Hall to hear sermons and discuss Buddhist doctrine. This is usually the only room in the monastery where lay practitioners are admitted, except perhaps for the libraries where Buddhist texts and scriptures are kept. In some traditions, however, monks always teach outdoors rather than in the monastery.

By early evening, all lay practitioners are gone, and the monks are free to read scripture and discuss various issues solely among themselves in the Sangha Hall. At certain times of the year, this is also where monks and nuns confess the ways in which they have strayed from the path toward enlightenment. These days are typically called "observance days," or *posadha*, and take place on days of a full or new moon. After all business in the Sangha Hall is finished for the day, participants retire to their individual sleeping quarters. In most monasteries, these small, relatively spartan cells make up a section of the monastery known as the Monks' Hall.

Many people view this simple lifestyle as easy, because it involves few demands and responsibilities. However, Thubten Chodron reports that it is not as easy at it might seem:

> If people become monks or nuns thinking to have an "easy life," their motivation is impure and they will not find ordained life satisfying. The causes of suffering —attachment, ignorance, and anger—follow us everywhere. They don't need a passport to go with us to another country, nor

are they left outside the monastery gates. If all we had to do to escape the hassles of life was to shave our head and put on robes, I think everyone would do it![38]

Life as a Lay Practitioner

Buddhists cloister themselves within monasteries and nunneries because they believe that doing so enables them to focus more wholly on their path to enlightenment. In fact, in some traditions—such as the Theravāda—it is considered impossible to reach enlightenment unless one enters into the monastic life. However, other Buddhists believe that lay practitioners have just as much opportunity to reach nirvana as any monk or nun has. For example, Thubten Chodron says,

Lay men and women can practice the Dharma in the same way as everyone else: by subduing their minds. In some Buddhist cultures, some people underestimate their potential by thinking, "I'm a lay person. Listening to teachings, chanting, and meditating are the work of monks and nuns. It's not my job. I just go to the temple, bow, make offerings, and pray for the welfare of my family." While these activities are good, lay people are capable of a rich spiritual life, in terms of both

learning Buddhism and integrating it into their daily life.[39]

The methods Buddhists use to achieve this integration vary. Generally, however, lay practitioners attend dharma talks led by monks and nuns, follow their five or eight Buddhist precepts, and meditate. Lay practitioners typically set a regular time for meditation, just as monks and nuns do. They might also meditate at other times of day as they wish.

There are two basic types of meditation among lay practitioners: stabilizing and analytical. Stabilizing meditation is meditation that develops concentration; analytical meditation is meditation that brings the practitioner insights. Each type of meditation is achieved through various techniques, depending on tradition and individual preference. The most common technique used in stabilizing meditation is to focus the mind on one's breathing without altering the rhythm of one's breaths. At the same time, the practitioner clears the mind of all thoughts. In stabilizing meditation, the practitioner, beginning from this clear state, focuses on a succession of single thoughts and directs the mind toward developing positive attitudes and understanding. For example, the practitioner might reflect on the impermanence of human life.

As part of meditation, a mantra may be chanted. Always recited in Sanskrit, the words of the mantras are believed to have been the words spoken by a buddha while in a deep state of meditation, and Buddhists generally believe that these words both produce positive energy and calm the mind. The most common mantra is *om mani padme hum*; it is particularly important in Tibetan Buddhism. Yet Buddhists disagree on the exact meaning of the phrase. It is literally translated as "Hail to the Jewel in the Lotus," with the lotus being the symbol of wisdom or enlightenment and the jewel referring to the teachings of the Buddha. Some Buddhists have suggested, however, that *om* refers to the goal of becoming a buddha; *mani,* the steps one must take to become a buddha; *padme,* the wisdom necessary to become a buddha; and *hum,* the collective mind of all who have already become buddhas. In this way, the

The Purpose of Meditation

There are many misconceptions about the purpose of meditation. Pema Chödrön, an American Tibetan Buddhist nun, tries to clear up some of these misconceptions in her essay "Loving-Kindness," in Samuel Bercholz and Sherab Chödzin Kohn's book An Introduction to the Buddha and His Teachings.

When people start to meditate or to work with any kind of spiritual discipline, they often think that somehow they're going to improve, which is a sort of subtle aggression against who they really are. It's a bit like saying, "If I jog, I'll be a much better person." "If I could only get a nicer house, I'd be a better person." "If I could meditate and calm down, I'd be a better person." Or the scenario might be that they find fault with others; they might say, "If it weren't for my husband, I'd have a perfect marriage." "If it weren't for the fact that my boss and I can't get on, my job would be just great." And "If it weren't for my mind, my meditation would be excellent." But meditation practice isn't about trying to throw ourselves away and become something better. It's about befriending who we are already. The ground of practice is you or me or whoever we are right now, just as we are. That's the ground, that's what we study, that's what we come to know with tremendous curiosity and interest.

phrase is believed to represent the elements necessary to attain enlightenment, and its constant repetition is thought to help a person focus on what is essential to achieve that goal.

The goal of meditation, not only in Tibetan Buddhism but in other forms of Buddhism as well, is to eliminate mental clutter in order to allow important truths to come forward. Psychologist David Fontana explains:

> Buddhist meditation teachers from all traditions instruct the practitioner to try and locate the point from which thoughts arise. As we try to do this in meditation, we come to recognize that thoughts arrive in the conscious mind suddenly, often taking us by surprise. Western psychology tells us they arise from the "unconscious"—a word used only to describe a process that we do not yet fully understand. Even experienced meditators may never be able to reach the point where they see thoughts actually forming, but at least we can recognize the point at which they enter our consciousness, rather than becoming aware of them only when they are fully formed.[40]

However, Fontana also notes that until a person becomes accustomed to meditation, it can be both boring and difficult. In advising beginning Buddhists, he says,

> Boredom can take many shapes and sizes. . . . Once the novelty of the first few days wears off meditation may seem flat and uninspiring, and the temptation to give up becomes strong. . . . Notice this restlessness and the way in which the mind is attempting to entice you away with its promise of more interesting activities, and remind yourself that the reason you meditate is precisely to learn how to overcome such tendencies.[41]

Beginning Buddhists typically find it easier to avoid such distractions if they meditate in a quiet, isolated place away from the concerns of daily life. To make this easier, some lay practitioners choose to live in a monastery for a short time in order to strengthen their concentration. In some Buddhist countries it is acceptable for a lay practitioner to become a monk for a short time, living in a monastery for anywhere from a few days to a year before returning to life as a lay practitioner. Many young men do this to develop mental and physical discipline in the most productive setting.

For Zen Buddhists, a modern alternative to the monastery for lay

A Buddhist nun participates in group zazen, *or meditation, as part of a* sesshin, *or retreat.*

practitioners is the retreat, or *sesshin.* Particularly popular in America, Zen retreats are periods of intensive Buddhist practice—usually seven days or longer—conducted by a Zen master. During the *sesshin,* participants are completely silent, except during interviews with the master. The typical *sesshin* starts at 4:30 A.M. each morning and ends at 10 P.M., with fifteen or more half-hour periods of group *zazen,* or meditation, during the day. In between these periods are ceremonies, meals, interviews with the master, teaching sessions, and rest and work periods. Rinzai Zen practitioners also spend a great deal of time considering various koans; Soto Zen practitioners have extra sessions of individual meditation, usually involving wall-gazing.

The Needs of Monks and Nuns

In addition to meditating, many lay practitioners in Buddhist countries spend time seeing to the needs of monks and nuns, providing them with food, clothing, and medicine. In many places, monks and nuns are strictly forbidden to handle money, so it is necessary for other people to conduct their business for them. The reason for this is twofold. First, it gives ordained Buddhists more chance to meditate and study so that they can become more effective teachers. Second, it forces monks and nuns to become involved with lay society rather than remaining isolated from it. Rupert Gethin, in his book *The Foundations of Buddhism*, explains:

It has sometimes been suggested that the Buddha originally intended to institute only a movement of committed ascetics removed from society; these are the true and original Buddhists.... [However,] the interaction of the monastic and lay communities is integral to the way of life set out by [early Buddhist texts]. Many of the rules of [these texts] concerned with food ... are clearly designed to force members of the Sangha to be dependent on lay support.... [For example,] a monk should not handle money; he should not eat food that he has not received from someone else; he should not dig the ground or have it dug, and so is effectively prohibited from farming; strictly he should not store food unless sick, and then only for seven days; finally he is discouraged from cooking. If called on to preach or attend to a lay supporter in various ways, then the community of monks should provide someone. All these rules have the effect of drawing the Buddhist monk into a relationship with society.[42]

Temples and Shrines

Lay practitioners also visit temples as a way to express their faith, even though no Buddhist dogma requires such visits. Buddhists visit temples at various times depending on tradition and personal preference. However, in Theravada Buddhism, lay practitioners typically visit a temple on the first, eighth, fifteenth, and twenty-third days of each lunar month; each of these days is known as an *uposatha*, or sacred day. During temple visits, whether on an *uposatha* or at some other time, lay practitioners often spend time meditating and perhaps also listening to a monk preach. In some traditions, temples are also places to pray and make offerings, either to the original Buddha or to all buddhas, depending on the tradition. Offerings might include flowers, incense, food, or water placed in beautiful bowls.

Such offerings might also be made in household shrines. These shrines usually include a statue of the Buddha and, again depending on tradition, statues of other buddhas, bodhisattvas, and deities. Tibetan Buddhists also sometimes place photographs of their spiritual teachers on their household shrines. In addition, some shrines contain Buddhist texts, small monuments (usually stupas), and Buddhist symbols such as the bell, which in some traditions represents the enlightened mind.

Whether in household shrines or in temples, most Buddhists bow down before images of the Buddha or buddhas as they worship. However, Buddhists insist that this does not mean they worship these images. Thubten Chodron explains:

Making an offering to the Buddha, a worshiper stands beside a shrine containing many statues of the Buddha, incense, and an offering of food.

A piece of clay, bronze, or jade is not the object of our respect and worship. . . . The [image] merely strengthens our memory. . . . When bowing before images of the Buddha, we recall the qualities of the enlightened beings and develop respect for their impartial love and compassion, generosity, ethical conduct, patience, joyous effort, concentration, and wisdom. The statue or painting reminds us of the qualities of the Buddhas, and we bow to those qualities, not to the clay. In fact, having a figure of the Buddha to bow before is not necessary. We can remember the Buddhas' qualities and develop respect without it.[43]

Prayers and Offerings

Similarly, Buddhists do not make offerings to the Buddha because they believe that the Buddha needs or wants them, nor do they do this to curry favor with the Buddha. In fact, in some traditions it is considered wrong to make an offering prior to asking the Buddha for something. Instead, Buddhist offerings are intended to show that Buddhists can do without material goods and to lessen their attachment to possessions. According to Chodron,

One purpose of making offerings is to pacify these harmful emotions of attachment and miserliness. Thus, when making an offering, we try to do so without any feelings of loss or regret. Water is readily accessible so that we can easily offer it without attachment or miserliness; bowls of water are often offered on the shrine. By offering with a happy mind, we habituate ourselves to the thought and action of giving. Thus we come to feel rich when we give and take pleasure in sharing good things with others.[44]

Offerings are also believed to be one way to accumulate merit, or credits for good deeds that are related to the Buddhist concept of karma. Buddhists also accumulate merit by meditating, listening to sutras, and donating money or goods to the Sangha. These credits are not tallied on earth; instead, they influence what type of rebirth a person will have in the next life. With enough credits, a person's next life will be a great improvement on the present one, thereby bringing that person closer to the attainment of enlightenment.

After an offering is made to the Buddha (or, in some traditions, the buddhas), he is said to take away the essence of that offering, as opposed to its physical form. This explains why the items remain on the shrine or at the temple until a monk or lay practitioner carries them away. Various offerings are generally believed to embody different elements of Buddhism. Incense, for example, represents ethics, while light represents wisdom and food represents the sustenance of meditation.

Food is also connected to Buddhist prayer. People pray before eating in order to reflect on all that went into creating and harvesting the food. In this way, Buddhists cultivate awareness. In addition, Buddhists pray to request help from the Buddha (or buddhas), either for themselves or for others. They might pray to become more patient or loving or to receive blessings, inspiration, or guidance from the Buddha, or they might petition the Buddha to heal or bring wealth to themselves or their loved ones. Some Buddhists believe that the Buddha does not answer such prayers and therefore do not say them. Others, however, believe that the Buddha does answer prayers that request things, provided that the petitioner takes certain actions to make the request likely to be granted. For example, if a person prays for better health yet practices a lifestyle in which the body is abused in some way, then the prayer is unlikely to be answered.

Buddhist Festivals and Ceremonies

In addition to meditation and prayer, religious festivals play an important role in the lives of many Buddhists. New Year's Day is a particularly important time for most Buddhists because it symbolizes death and rebirth, the essence of Buddhist teachings. New Year's rituals vary according to country and tradition, but generally they involve purification—some kind of cleansing ceremony, usually incorporating water—and meditation.

Buddhists in many countries also celebrate important events in the life of the Buddha with festivals. On such days, people might bring special offerings to Buddhist temples, where they then meditate and pray. They also sometimes take part in public celebrations. For example, in Laos the Buddha's birth is honored by pouring holy water on all statues of the Buddha, after which people pour water on themselves and each other as well. They also release trapped fish into the rivers and caged birds into the sky to celebrate the freedom that comes from enlightenment. In Japan, tea instead of water is poured over the Buddha's statues; this practice stems from the belief that the first tea plants sprang from the Buddha's blood.

In countries where Theravāda Buddhism predominates, the Buddha's birth, enlightenment, and death (or, rather, his attainment of nirvāna) are all believed to have occurred in the month of May during a full moon. Consequently, every May the day of the full moon brings many celebrations, including religious processions and plays about the life of the Buddha.

There are also many religious ceremonies in Buddhism, although they too vary according to tradition. For example, in countries where Theravāda predominates, babies are taken at birth to the local temple, where they are blessed by a monk and sprinkled with holy water. As part of this ceremony, hot wax from a candle is dripped into a bowl of water to symbolize the joining of earth, air, fire, and water. Some traditions have similar ceremonies related to marriage, but in others monks are forbidden to attend weddings.

There are, however, many elaborate ceremonies related to death and funerals, largely because Buddhists view death as an important transition that might eventually lead to nirvana. Monks might recite sermons over the newly deceased, anoint the body with water, and/or burn incense during funerals, cremations, and postcremation dinners to honor the deceased. In

Buddhist monks receive holy water at a cleansing ceremony.

Religious accessories, such as these bells, beads, and incense burner vary greatly among Buddhists.

some traditions, monks are invited to eat meals in the deceased's household for many days after the funeral and cremation in order to accumulate merit posthumously for a person who might not have done enough good deeds during his or her lifetime. However, as with other Buddhist practices, the variety of death-related rituals is great.

Variety in Practices

The reason for this variety is that the Buddha did not provide his disciples with specific religious rituals to perform. Without guidelines, his followers felt free to develop such rituals as they pleased, and individuals in different parts of the world came up with different practices. Perhaps the widest variety is in the type of clothing worn

while worshiping, as well as in religious "accessories" such as statues, incense burners, bells, and gongs.

Some Buddhists accept this variety as an essential part of Buddhism. For example, Tibetan Buddhist nun Thubten Chodron says, "As the Buddha's teachings spread from one country to another, they adapted to the culture and mentality of the people in each place without changing the essential meaning. The style of [a monk's] robes is an external form, not the actual internal meaning of the teaching, thus it may change."[45] Others, however, have problems with the fact that Buddhists have developed a variety of practices, believing that they create many misconceptions about the nature of Buddhism. Steve Hagan says,

Rituals, ceremonies, prayers, and special outfits are inevitable, but they do not—they cannot—express the heart of what the Buddha taught. In fact, all too often, such things get in the way. They veil the simple wisdom of the Buddha's words, and distract us from it. This is a major problem, and not just for those of us raised in the West. It is not easy to know where Buddhism ends and Asian culture begins, or to distinguish the original and authentic teachings of the Buddha from what was added later by people with less acute insight. As a result, many Americans and Europeans genuinely believe that Buddhism is about worshipping Buddha, or bowing and wearing robes, or working oneself into a trance, or coming up with answers to bewildering riddles, or past and future incarnations.[46]

In spite of the variations in practice, the essential message of Buddhism remains the same. Increasingly, that message resonates with people in parts of the world never previously touched by Buddhism.

chapter | seven

Western Buddhism

Westerners' first knowledge of Buddhism came around the beginning of the third century B.C. after a Greek named Megasthenes mentioned the religion in an account he wrote of his visit to India. Shortly thereafter, the Greeks began trading with India and other Buddhist countries, and Roman traders soon followed suit. Western exposure to Buddhism increased as Europeans began trading with and colonizing Asia in the fifteenth century. Yet Westerners were little concerned with learning about Buddhism.

Western attitudes changed in the nineteenth century when several serious scholars undertook the task of translating Buddhist texts. Just as their works were being published, Western archaeologists were finding the ruins of Buddhist temples in India and other Asian countries. These discoveries increased interest in Buddhism not only among scholars but among the European public as well. This interest was nurtured by an increasing disaffection with Christianity, which made Europeans receptive to new religions and philosophies. At the same time, science was coming to be seen as having more value than religion when it came to determining truth, and Western society began to suffer from what scholar John Snelling calls a "spiritual vacuum."[47]

The discovery of ruins such as this Buddhist monastery in Tibet increased Western and European interest in Buddhist beliefs.

Adding Occult Elements

Many Westerners started looking for a way to fill that vacuum. One of the most popular ways was through the practice of spiritualism and occultism, but soon Buddhism gained Europeans' attention as well. In 1879, after Sir Edwin Arnold published an epic poem about the Buddha, *The Light of Asia*, there was a sudden burst of interest in the Buddha's teachings. Several prominent Russian, German, American, and British religious leaders and philosophers, having read *The Light of Asia*, converted to Buddhism and promoted the religion among their followers.

However, they also blended their own ideas into Buddhist doctrine. For example, some Westerners combined elements of occultism with their Buddhist practices, including the first Westerner to become a dedicated Buddhist monk, Allan Bennett (1872–1923). Bennett was a member of a British occult group called the Hermetic Order of the Golden Dawn, and this group apparently funded his trip to Sri Lanka and Burma to study the dharma. Similarly, in the United States, New England philosophers such as Henry David Thoreau incorporated elements of Buddhism into Transcendentalism, a philosophy that included the idea that there are two levels of reality. Later, Thoreau promoted Buddhism by translating a French version of the *Lotus Sūtra* into English. Other people promoted Buddhism by arranging for Asian Buddhists of various schools to come to the United States to speak.

Zen Influence

Western interest in Buddhism increased greatly in the latter half of the twentieth century. During the twentieth century, two devastating world wars fostered in many Westerners a revulsion for violence. Since nonviolence is the essence of Buddhism, the religion gained many followers in the Western world. Among the most prominent was British lawyer and author Travers Christmas Humphreys (1901–1983),

who is credited with leading a British Buddhist movement. The type of Buddhism that Humphreys promoted was Zen, and one of his followers, Alan Watts (1915–1973) carried his enthusiasm for this school to the United States. Here, Watts wrote and lectured extensively on Buddhism for many years.

Another prominent promoter of Zen in the United States was Suzuki Daisetu Teitaro (1870–1966), who became known in America as D. T. Suzuki. As a young man, he came to the United States from Japan to translate Japanese Buddhist texts into

Tibetan Gurus

During the 1940s and '50s, many Westerners sought out Tibetan gurus in their native land to learn about Buddhism without really understanding what kind of challenge the religion could be. The following story, related to John Snelling by an Englishman who sought out a guru in southern Tibet in 1947, is a common one.

We had to walk a long way to find [the guru]. He himself was a recluse: he lived in a little hut. The first time we met, he said, "Well, now, it's best that you should have the bases," and he produced this large loose-leaved book. "Now, you learn that by heart and when you know it we'll start." Well, I conveyed to him that for us this was something very difficult. "Oh, it's not difficult at all," he said; so I said, "We'll try." And the next time we went, he said, "I've thought about what you've said and so I've found another book which is really the same book reduced to a small formula—a few pages. This you must at all costs learn by heart." We did learn it and after a few days we recited it to him correctly. He said, "That's a good beginning."

English. Eventually, he turned to writing and lecturing about Zen Buddhism in a way Americans could easily understand. Suzuki's books were the first popular works on Zen to be published in the United States. Many people therefore credit him with inspiring a Zen movement in America.

The late 1950s and '60s were a time of further growth for Buddhism in the United States. During these decades, young Americans, disillusioned with Western religions' seeming inability to promote peace, increasingly turned to Eastern religions in general and Buddhism in particular.

Western Zen

By the early 1970s, many Buddhist training centers and retreats had been founded across the United States, with the largest concentration along the West Coast. One of the best known Buddhist training centers established during this period was the San Francisco Zen Center. Its master, a Soto Zen Buddhist named Shunryu Suzuki (1904–1971), wrote an extremely popular book titled *Zen Mind, Beginner's Mind*, which immediately became a best-seller and attracted many Americans to Zen Buddhism. Moreover, Suzuki's Zen Center promoted the establishment of

Americans who are attracted to Buddhism study at training centers like the San Francisco Zen Center.

other facilities dedicated to teaching Zen Buddhism, including the first monastery established in the United States.

In the last two decades of the twentieth century, Buddhism and Buddhist values increasingly appealed to Americans who felt guilt over lifestyles that seemed extremely lavish in comparison with those in other parts of the world. Many Americans turned to Zen Buddhism after deciding that their desire for more and better material possessions was shallow, because Zen Buddhism promotes the idea that only a simple lifestyle encumbered by few possessions will allow someone to achieve enlightenment.

For Westerners who embrace Buddhism, however, there are many challenges. For example, the call of the material world and the need to earn a living present a continuing problem for American Buddhists who wish to be part of the Sangha. Whereas in the East monks and nuns are supported by lay practitioners and thus do not need paying jobs, in the West there is rarely such lay support. Therefore, most Western Zen Buddhist monks must work, usually at fairly ordinary jobs, and as a result most Zen centers are located in towns and cities where work is available rather than in remote areas where worldly distractions are less of a concern.

In addition to accommodating the need to earn a living, Buddhism in the West has had to change some long-standing practices to reflect Western values. In particular, Western feminism has led to the abandonment of certain sexist Asian Buddhist practices. For example, in the Far East, male and female Buddhists are not considered equal, even though both are considered capable of achieving enlightenment. Buddhist nuns there must always defer to Buddhist monks, and in some Southeast Asian countries, there have been no fully ordained nuns for centuries because of a lack of support for female Buddhists. In the West, however, men and women are trained equally in Zen, have the same status, can achieve the same goals, and are involved in many important activities within the Zen center.

Some Zen centers have tried to make Buddhism more palatable to Westerners in other ways as well, by eliminating aspects of the religion that are strongly Asian. David Scott and Tony Doubleday, in their book *The Elements of Zen*, explain:

The extent to which Western Zen should adopt the Far Eastern trappings in which Zen is "packaged" has been treated in widely differing ways. Some Western lineages have made every effort to remove all vestiges of the oriental origins of the practice. Thus all the terms of reference, the Sutras and chants have been translated into near-European equivalents, and forms of presentation have been adopted from the European religious traditions. . . . The motives for making or refraining from making any changes to the oriental treatment of Zen will be tested in the fullness of time; some will emerge as successful, others will be disregarded as inappropriate. For the time being, the choice of teaching styles and traditions available to the beginner is wide.[48]

Many Zen Buddhist masters, however, find it difficult to make Buddhism easier for Westerners, who sometimes struggle more with its disciplined practices than Asians do. Zen Buddhist Dogen Zenji once advised his American followers,

Even people in the secular world must concentrate on one thing and learn it thoroughly enough to be able to do it in front of others rather than learn many things at the same time, without truly accomplishing any of them. . . . Students concentrate on one thing.[49]

American Buddhists, however, are so accustomed to doing many things at once that they often cannot achieve the level of mental focus their religion demands.

Nichiren Buddhism

For some in the West, Zen's demands simply are impossible to meet, but other Buddhist traditions are more accessible. For example, the Nichiren sect of Buddhism, known as Nichiren Shoshu in the West, encourages Americans to maintain their accustomed lavish lifestyles. In particular, Nichiren appeals to celebrities and wealthy people who do not want to abandon their excessive lifestyles or feel guilty about them. John Snelling explains:

Nichiren Shoshu has taken on remarkably [in recent years], noticeably among many younger people whom in the usual course would not be expected to be attracted to Buddhism, such as stars of show business. Part of its appeal may lie in the fact that it does not disparage this-worldly success. Newcomers are encouraged to chant for what they want in terms of money, material goods, job success, and the fulfillment of other personal desires. On the face of it, this looks a very un-Buddhist approach. . . .

However, within the movement things are viewed differently. There, desire is recognized as having positive uses; in particular it can be used to demonstrate the power of spiritual practice, and this in itself can have a profoundly transformative effect.[50]

Nichiren Buddhism is also attractive to minorities. By some estimates, of the 50,000 to 150,000 followers of Nichiren Buddhism in the United States, roughly 25 to 30 percent are African American or Hispanic. For these people, the religion has an important message apart from its allowance for Western materialism. Dr. Charles Johnson, a philosopher and prominent African American writer who is also a Buddhist, discusses this message in terms of his own family's experiences with Nichiren Buddhism (also known as Sōka Gakkai):

Soka Gakkai's initial attraction for [black Americans] came about because they discovered that through chanting they could transform their lives and, in fact, that they alone were the architects of their own suffering and happiness. For my sister-in-law, raised Baptist and impoverished in a housing project on Chicago's South Side, the black church with its white Jesus had always been an unsatisfying experience, one from which she felt emotionally distant since childhood; for her friend, a woman raised as a Catholic, Soka Gakkai provided—through its explanation of karma and reincarnation and its foundation in the *Lotus Sutra*—a reason for the individual suffering she saw in the world, convincing her this was not due to the will of God but instead was based causally on each person's actions in this life and previous ones. Global peace is their goal. Chanting is their tool for self-transformation, empowerment, and experiencing the at-oneness with being they both had sought all their lives....Many white Buddhists new to the Zen and Tibetan traditions dismiss Soka Gakkai for what they consider its skewed, Christian-oriented, materialistic version of Buddhism. For me, Soka Gakkai is but one branch on the Bodhi tree. Yet its success in recruiting black Americans indicates that people of color find in Buddhism the depths

of their long-denied humanity . . . and a path (the Eightfold Path) for a moral and civilized way of life.[51]

Tibetan Buddhism

If Western lifestyles present a challenge to Buddhism, the faith appears willing to accept that challenge. In particular, Tibetan Buddhism emphasizes the need to integrate Buddhism into daily life. Lectures and writings by Tibetan Buddhists in the West stress the importance of learning about all Buddhist teachings and applying this knowledge to everyday activities. The American lectures of the Dalai Lama, for example, often

The Dalai Lama's American lectures, like this one held in Wisconsin, help people see how they can apply Buddhism to daily life.

Tibetan-Style Therapy

Psychotherapists are increasingly incorporating elements of Buddhism into their sessions with patients. In discussing how she uses Tibetan Buddhism in her own practice, psychologist Karen Kissel Wegela, in a May 2001 article for Shambhala Sun *magazine titled "No Family Picnic," says that "the* lojong *teachings, brought to Tibet from India by the Buddhist teacher Atisha, give us some wonderful guidelines in the form of a series of pithy slogans." One of her favorites is "Abandon any hope of fruition," which she shares with her patients in order to teach them to "forget about attaining perfection."*

Often I see folks in therapy who feel disappointed in themselves and discouraged when they see that they are still doing the same old things. . . . Instead of regarding our lack of progress as a problem, we can appreciate the clarity we now have about the work we still need to do. . . . Many of the [Tibetan Buddhist] slogans point us toward the importance of letting our hearts soften. We could be gentle to ourselves and to those we find so challenging. The practice of sitting meditation, and the Mahāyāna practice of exchanging ourselves with others [i.e., showing compassion], provide us with time-tested ways to cultivate our hearts.

help people see how they can adapt Buddhism to their personal needs. According to Buddhists Geshe Thupten Jinpa and Richard Barron (also known as Chökyi Nyima),

One factor to which His Holiness [the Dalai Lama] returns again and again is the importance, for a practitioner, of a wider knowledge of the whole structure of the Buddhist teaching. Hand in hand with this, he underlines the need to learn how to interpret the specific terminology used in the different schools and strata of Buddhism. And at the same time as he insists on a more rigorous approach to studying the sources of Buddhism, His Holiness loses no opportunity to provide clues and instructions on how to apply specific points to the everyday business of living.[52]

Psychotherapy

Buddhists are willing to engage the Western world and work to apply their values to everyday life. For some,

Buddhism provides direct, practical benefits. For example, Western psychologists and psychiatrists have long integrated Buddhist principles and practices into their therapy sessions with patients, because in essence the goals of Buddhism and psychotherapy are the same. Psychotherapists aim to help their patients identify their causes of suffering so they can heal themselves, much as Buddhists examine their own suffering so they can become self-aware and achieve enlightenment.

In his book *The Feeling Buddha*, David Brazier explains the similarities between Buddhism and psychotherapy:

> To examine the feeling while in the feeling, as the Buddha says, is the key to effective psychotherapy. Therapy provides a kind of ritual in which a space is created where it is possible for feelings to be contained. The boundaries of the therapy relationship act as a protective embankment. The space inside becomes a place where the client [patient] feels safe to explore what seem like dangerous issues without so much fear. It is a place where the client can learn to handle their fire without getting burnt. There is a direct parallel between contemporary psychological practice and the Buddha's

advocacy of containment and protection as the necessary conditions for psychological transformation.[53]

In other words, Brazier sees a parallel between "taking refuge in the Buddha"—cloistering oneself in a monastery to focus on important personal growth—and taking refuge in a psychotherapist's office to work through important personal issues. However, he also notes that, whereas psychotherapy is only attempting to achieve small changes in a person's behavior and thinking, Buddhism seeks to effect a major change in a person as well as "the renewal of civilization through the work of transformed individuals"[54] (i.e., the buddhas).

With Zen Buddhism's introduction into the United States after World War II, psychologists who had studied the writings of Zen scholar D. T. Suzuki noted the connection between the goal of achieving enlightenment and the goal of freeing the unconscious mind. According to Suzuki, the aim of Zen was to develop

> the art of seeing into the nature of one's being, and it points the way from bondage to freedom. . . . We can say that Zen liberates all the energies properly and naturally stored in each of us, which are in ordinary circumstances cramped

and distorted so that they find no adequate channel of activity.... It is the object of Zen, therefore, to save us from going crazy or being crippled. This is what I mean by freedom, giving free play to all the creative and benevolent impulses inherently lying in our hearts. Generally, we are blind to this fact, that we are in possession of all the necessary faculties that will make us happy and loving towards one another.[55]

In connecting Suzuki's words to the practice of psychotherapy, psychiatrist Erich Fromm asserted that Suzuki's description of Zen's goal "could be applied without change as a description of what psychoanalysis aspires to achieve."[56]

Once this connection had been recognized, psychotherapists began to employ meditation techniques in their therapy sessions to lessen control of the ego, and today the use of meditation in therapy is commonplace. However, this practice has not been without controversy. In the 1980s, psychologist Ken Wilbur warned that in people with certain mental illnesses, a strong ego is necessary in order to keep the person functioning in society. In fact, Wilbur suggested that even people in the West who are not suffering from mental illness

are unprepared to free themselves from the ego as Buddhism intends them to do. Other psychologists have expressed similar views, doubting whether Americans are suited for the most intense level of Buddhist practices.

Nonetheless, interest in the most demanding aspects of Buddhism continues to rise among Westerners. This includes a lifelong commitment to Buddhist practices and perhaps even monastery life. Rupert Gethin, in his book *The Foundations of Buddhism*, reports,

> The number of Westerners ordaining into Theravada, Tibetan, and East Asian Sanghas and living as monks both in Asia and the West has increased significantly in the last twenty-five years; in Buddhist circles in the West it is not uncommon to find Westerners with thirty or forty years of involvement with Buddhist practice behind them; some Westerners have gained an authority as teachers which is recognized by Asian Buddhists. The overall numbers of committed practitioners may still be relatively small, but the growth of interest among Westerners in Buddhism since the Second World War is a significant feature of religious practice in the West.[57]

Buddhist monks translate important points of a Buddhist ceremony to Western pilgrims seeking enlightenment in eastern India.

In turning to Buddhism, many Westerners are heartened by the fact that the Buddha taught that enlightenment is attainable by all. Moreover, they believe that Buddhism has much to offer the modern world, including a compassionate live-and-let-live philosophy that promotes altruism and global peace. And because Buddhism is continually adapting itself to new circumstances, ideas, and cultures, chances are good that it will remain a thriving religion in the future.

Notes

Introduction: A Growing Religion

1. Thubten Chodron, *Buddhism for Beginners*. Ithaca, NY: Snow Lion Publications, 2001, p. 77.
2. Steve Hagan, *Buddhism Plain and Simple*. New York: Broadway Books, 1999, pp. 8–9.
3. Chögyam Trungpa Rinpoche, "The Decision to Become a Buddhist," *Shambhala Sun*, May 2001, p. 32.

Chapter One: The Origins of Buddhism

4. E. J. Thomas, *The Life of the Buddha*. London: Kegan Paul, 1949, p. 31.
5. Quoted in John Snelling, *The Buddhist Handbook*. New York: Barnes & Noble Books, 1991, p. 21.
6. Snelling, *The Buddhist Handbook*, p. 21.
7. Snelling, *The Buddhist Handbook*, p. 22.
8. Andrew Skilton, *A Concise History of Buddhism*. New York: Barnes & Noble Books, 2000, pp. 25–26.

Chapter Two: The Teachings of the Buddha

9. Thich Nhat Hanh, *The Heart of the Buddha's Teachings*. New York: Broadway Books, 1999, p. 13.
10. Hanh, *The Heart of the Buddha's Teachings*, p. 15.

11. Quoted in Rupert Gethin, *The Foundations of Buddhism*. Oxford, England: Oxford University Press, 1998, p. 29.
12. Hagan, *Buddhism Plain and Simple*, pp. 25-26.
13. Quoted in Samuel Bercholz and Sherab Chödzin Kohn, eds., *An Introduction to the Buddha and His Teachings*. New York: Barnes & Noble Books, 1997, p. 62.
14. Hanh, *The Heart of the Buddha's Teachings*, p. 19.
15. Quoted in Bercholz and Kohn, *An Introduction to the Buddha and His Teachings*, pp. 62-63.
16. Quoted in Bercholz and Kohn, *An Introduction to the Buddha and His Teachings*, p. 63.
17. Hanh, *The Heart of the Buddha's Teachings*, pp. 22–23.
18. Snelling, *The Buddhist Handbook*, p. 52.
19. Snelling, *The Buddhist Handbook*, p. 26.
20. Quoted in Skilton, *A Concise History of Buddhism*, p. 40.
21. Quoted in Skilton, *A Concise History of Buddhism*, p. 24.
22. Quoted in Skilton, *A Concise History of Buddhism*, p. 61.

Chapter Three: The Development of Buddhism in India

23. Skilton, *A Consise History of Buddhism*, p. 46.

24. Quoted in Gethin, *The Foundations of Buddhism*, p. 38.
25. Gethin, *The Foundations of Buddhism*, pp. 36–37.
26. Gethin, *The Foundations of Buddhism*, p. 36.
27. Quoted in Snelling, *The Buddhist Handbook,* p. 31.
28. Skilton, *A Consise History of Buddhism*, p. 61.
29. Quoted in Snelling, *The Buddhist Handbook*, p. 79.

Chapter Four: The Spread of Buddhism

30. Gethin, *The Foundations of Buddhism*, p. 202.
31. Gethin, *The Foundations of Buddhism*, p. 204.
32. Quoted in Gethin, *The Foundations of Buddhism*, p. 229.

Chapter Five: Two Unique Paths: Tibetan and Japanese Buddhism

33. Snelling, *The Buddhist Handbook*, pp. 98–99.
34. Skilton, *A Concise History of Buddhism*, p. 179.
35. Quoted in David Scott and Tony Doubleday, *The Elements of Zen*. New York: Barnes & Noble Books, 1997, p. 56.
36. David Fontana, *Discover Zen*. San Francisco: Chronicle Books, 2001, p. 104.

Chapter Six: Buddhist Practices

37. Chodron, *Buddhism for Beginners*, p. 117.
38. Chodron, *Buddhism for Beginners*, pp. 119–20.
39. Chodron, *Buddhism for Beginners*, p. 118.
40. Fontana, *Discover Zen*, p. 78.
41. Fontana, *Discover Zen*, p. 87.
42. Gethin, *The Foundations of Buddhism*, pp. 93–94.
43. Chodron, *Buddhism for Beginners*, pp. 137–38.
44. Chodron, *Buddhism for Beginners*, pp. 138–39.
45. Chodron, *Buddhism for Beginners*, p. 77.
46. Hagan, *Buddhism Plain and Simple*, pp. 3-4.

Chapter Seven: Western Buddhism

47. Snelling, *The Buddhist Handbook*, p. 195.
48. Scott and Doubleday, *The Elements of Zen*, p. 24.
49. Quoted in Scott and Doubleday, *The Elements of Zen*, pp. 24–25.
50. Snelling, *The Buddhist Handbook*, p. 219.
51. Charles Johnson, "A Sangha by Another Name," *Tricycle: The Buddhist Review*, Winter 1999, pp. 110-111.
52. Quoted in His Holiness the Dalai Lama, *Dzogchen: The Heart Essence of*

the Great Perfection. Trans. Geshe Thupten Jinpa and Richard Barron. Ed. Patrick Gaffney. Ithaca, NY: Snow Lion Publications, 2000, p. 16.

53. David Brazier, *The Feeling Buddha*, New York: Fromm International, 1998, p. 108.

54. Brazier, *The Feeling Buddha*, p. 105.

55. Quoted in Snelling, *The Buddhist Handbook*, p. 250.

56. Quoted in Snelling, *The Buddhist Handbook*, p. 250.

57. Gethin, *The Foundations of Buddhism*, p. 275.

For Further Reading

Gary Gach and Michael Wenger, *The Complete Idiot's Guide to Understanding Buddhism.* New York: Alpha Books, 2001. This book is a simple and comprehensive guide to Buddhism in its many forms.

Geshe Kelsang Gyatso, *Joyful Path of Good Fortune: The Complete Guide to the Buddhist Path to Enlightenment.* Seattle, WA: Tharpa Publications, 1996. Written by an expert in Mahāyāna Buddhism, this book presents the teachings and meditations of Mahāyāna Buddhism in general and a type of Mahāyāna Buddhism known as the lamrim tradition in particular.

Geshe Kelsang Gyatso, *A Meditation Handbook: A Step-by-Step Manual, Providing a Clear, Practical Guide to Buddhist Meditation.* Seattle, WA: Tharpa Publications, 1995. This guide to Buddhist meditation techniques includes twenty-one increasingly complex meditations of the Buddhist Path to Enlightenment, commonly practiced by Tibetan Buddhists.

Donald S. Lopez Jr., *The Story of Buddhism: A Concise Guide to Its History and Teachings.* San Francisco, CA: Harper San Francisco, 2001. Written by a professor of Buddhist studies at the University of Michigan, this book offers clear, in-depth discussions of various topics related to Buddhism, such as monastic life and pilgrimage.

Jack Hosho Maguire, *Essential Buddhism: A Complete Guide to Beliefs and Practices.* New York: Pocket Books, 2001. Written by a monk of the Mountains and Rivers Order in New York, this book discusses the life of the Buddha, compares Buddhism to other religions, and clearly explains various aspects of Buddhist beliefs, teachings, and practices.

Gary McClain and Eve Adams, *The Complete Idiot's Guide to Zen Living.* New York: Alpha Books, 2000. This book is a beginner's guide to Zen Buddhism that offers ways to integrate Buddhism into Western life.

Dinty W. Moore, *The Accidental Buddhist: Mindfulness, Enlightenment, and Sitting Still.* Chapel Hill, NC: Algonquin Books, 1997. This book recounts the experiences of a journalist and filmmaker who traveled throughout the United States as part of a personal quest to discover how Buddhism is practiced in America.

C. Alexander Simpkins, and Annellen Simpkins, *Simple Buddhism: A Guide to Enlightened Living.* Boston, MA: Charles E. Tuttle, 2000. Written by two psychologists, this guide to Buddhism offers basic information on the history, themes, and meditation principles and techniques of Buddhism.

Jean Smith, *The Beginner's Guide to Zen Buddhism.* New York: Bell Tower, 2000. Intended for people who want to practice Zen Buddhism but have had no experience with it, this book discusses the basics regarding meditation postures, clothing, and techniques as well as Zen Buddhist teachings.

Works Consulted

Books

Samuel Bercholz and Sherab Chödzin Kohn, eds., *An Introduction to the Buddha and His Teachings*. New York: Barnes & Noble Books, 1997. This book offers a collection of essays by leading Buddhists practicing a variety of traditions.

Sandy Boucher, *Opening the Lotus: A Woman's Guide to Buddhism*. Boston: Beacon Press, 1997. Written by a longtime Buddhist practitioner, this book is a basic guide to Buddhism from a woman's perspective.

David Brazier, *The Feeling Buddha*. New York: Fromm International, 1998. This book by a psychotherapist talks about Buddhism in terms of its emotional and psychological aspects.

Thubten Chodron, *Buddhism for Beginners*. Ithaca, NY: Snow Lion Publications, 2001. Written by a Tibetan Buddhist nun, this book uses a question-and-answer approach to explain various aspects of Buddhism in general and Tibetan Buddhism in particular.

David Fontana, *Discover Zen*. San Francisco: Chronicle Books, 2001. Written by a British psychologist who teaches at the Cardiff University in Wales, this book is a basic guide to the principles and practices of Zen Buddhism.

Lene Gammelgaard, *Climbing High*. NY: HarperCollins, 1999. Lene Gammelgaard describes her experiences with Tibetan Buddhists while discussing her climb up Mount Everest.

Rupert Gethin, *The Foundations of Buddhism*. Oxford, England: Oxford University Press, 1998. Written by an expert in Indian religions who practices Theravāda Buddhism, this book offers clear explanations of the Buddha's teachings and the common elements among Buddhist traditions.

Steve Hagan, *Buddhism Plain and Simple*. New York: Broadway Books, 1999. This basic guidebook simplifies Buddhist teachings for beginners.

Thich Nhat Hanh, *The Heart of the Buddha's Teachings*. New York: Broadway Books, 1999. Written by a Vietnamese Buddhist monk who is a popular lecturer and author of books on Buddhism, this work introduces the core teachings of Buddhism and how they relate to daily life.

His Holiness the Dalai Lama, *Dzogchen: The Heart Essence of the Great Perfection*. Trans. Geshe Thupten Jinpa and Richard Barron. Ed. Patrick Gaffney. Ithaca, NY: Snow Lion Publications, 2000. This book is a collection of lectures given by the Dalai Lama, the spiritual leader of Tibetan Buddhists, in the West from 1982 to 1989.

David Scott and Tony Doubleday, *The Elements of Zen*. New York: Barnes & Noble Books, 1997. This simple guidebook introduces the core teachings of Zen Buddhism.

Andrew Skilton, *A Concise History of Buddhism*. New York: Barnes & Noble Books, 2000. This lengthy work traces the history of Buddhism throughout the world.

John Snelling, *The Buddhist Handbook*. New York: Barnes & Noble Books, 1991. This book is a complete guide to Buddhist schools, teachings, and practices.

E. J. Thomas, *The Life of the Buddha*. London: Kegan Paul, 1949. This book offers details about the Buddha's life.

Periodicals

Charles Johnson, "A Sangha by Another Name," *Tricycle: The Buddhist Review*, Winter 1999.

Chögyam Trungpa Rinpoche, "The Decision to Become a Buddhist," *Shambhala Sun*, May 2001.

Karen Kissel Wegela, "No Family Picnic," *Shambhala Sun*, May 2001.

Index

Picture Credits

About the Author

Patricia D. Netzley received a bachelor's degree in English from the University of California at Los Angeles (UCLA). After graduation she worked as an editor at the UCLA Medical Center, where she produced hundreds of medical articles, speeches, and pamphlets. Her hobbies are weaving, knitting, and needlework. She and her husband, Raymond, live in southern California with their children, Matthew, Sarah, and Jacob.